RELIGION AND FAITH IN AFRICA

RELIGION AND FAITH IN AFRICA

Confessions of an Animist

AGBONKHIANMEGHE E. OROBATOR, SJ

ORBIS BOOKS
www.orbisbooks.com

ORBIS BOOKS
Maryknoll, New York 10545

Fathers and Brothers
MARYKNOLL™

Founded in 1970, Orbis Books endeavors to publish works that enlighten the mind, nourish the spirit, and challenge the conscience. The publishing arm of the Maryknoll Fathers and Brothers, Orbis seeks to explore the global dimensions of the Christian faith and mission, to invite dialogue with diverse cultures and religious traditions, and to serve the cause of reconciliation and peace. The books published reflect the views of their authors and do not represent the official position of the Maryknoll Society. To learn more about Maryknoll and Orbis Books, please visit our website at www.maryknollsociety.org.

Library of Congress Cataloging-in-Publication Data

Names: Orobator, A. E. author.
Title: Religion and faith in Africa : confessions of an animist / Agbonkhianmeghe E. Orobator, SJ.
Description: Maryknoll : Orbis Books, 2018. | Includes bibliographical references and index.
Identifiers: LCCN 2017052748 (print) | LCCN 2017057805 (ebook) | ISBN 9781608337422 (e-book) | ISBN 9781626982765 (pbk.)
Subjects: LCSH: Christianity—Africa. | Christianity and other religions. | Religions—Relations.
Classification: LCC BR1360 (ebook) | LCC BR1360 .O76 2018 (print) | DDC 276—dc23
LC record available at http://lcco.loc.gov/2017052748

To Baba and Mama

Contents

Series Foreword

Duffy Lectures in Global Christianity

Catherine Cornille

Never, in the history of Christianity, has Christian faith been expressed in so many forms. While long a global religion, it is only in the course of the twentieth century that the church came to valorize and celebrate the particularity of the different cultures and that local churches were creatively encouraged to engage and appropriate indigenous symbols, categories, and modes of celebration. A milestone in the Catholic Church was the 1975 apostolic exhortation *Evangelii nuntiandi*, which states:

> The individual Churches, intimately built up not only of people but also of aspirations, of riches and limitations, of ways of praying, of loving, of looking at life and the world, which distinguish this or that human gathering, have the task of assimilating the essence of the Gospel message and of transposing it, without the slightest betrayal of its essential truth, into the language that these particular people understand, then of proclaiming it in this language. (no. 63)

The term language is here understood in the broad anthropological and cultural sense to touch upon not only translation of the gospel message, but also "liturgical expression . . .

catechesis, theological formulation, secondary ecclesial structures, and ministries" (no. 63). It thus involves a thorough rethinking of the gospel in terms and structures resonant with particular cultures, and a focus on the social, political, and spiritual questions and challenges alive in those cultures.

The notions of inculturation and contextualization have since become firmly engrained in Christian theological thinking. One has come to speak of Latino/a theology, African theology, Indian theology, and so forth, each giving way to even more local or focused theologies, such as Igbo theology, Mestizo theology, or Dalit theology. This raises questions about the relationship among all of these forms of theologizing and about the relationship between the individual and the universal church.

The goal of inculturation and indigenous theologies in the first place is, of course, to better serve the local churches and to respond to their particular needs and questions. But many of the cultural riches mined in the process of inculturation may also become a source of inspiration for other churches or for what is called the universal church. *Evangelii nuntiandi* clearly warns, "Let us be very careful not to conceive of the universal Church as the sum, or, if one can say so, the more or less anomalous federation of essentially different churches" (no. 62). It implores individual churches to remain in communion with the universal church. But it does not yet fully appreciate the opportunity for the universal church to learn from local churches. There is still an often unspoken assumption that theological models and currents that have developed in Europe remain normative and that local theologies are but various forms of expression of the same theological insights. However, all theology (including Western theology) entails both universal and culturally particular dimensions, and each attempt to express the gospel within a particular culture may bring out new dimensions of its message relevant for all believers. As the center of gravity of the church is shifting, and as the distinction between local and universal or global is becoming more blurred, it is becoming more than ever important and possible for different theological traditions to engage and enrich one another. This is why the department of theology at Boston College established the Duffy Chair in Global Christianity. Each year a theologian from a different continent is invited to deliver a series of lectures dealing with the theological challenges and insights arising from his or her particular context. These challenges and insights may focus on ethical questions, theological developments, biblical hermeneutics, spiritual and ritual practices, and so on. The goal is not only to inform faculty and students of the ways in which theology is done in particular parts of the world, but also to raise new questions and offer new insights that might enrich local theological reflection in North America and beyond. The department is very pleased to partner with Orbis Books in order to make the fruit of this theological reflection more broadly available.

The Duffy Chair in Global Christianity was named after Father Stephen J. Duffy (1931–2007), who taught systematic theology at Loyola University in New Orleans from 1971 to 2007, and who was himself deeply engaged with questions of religious and cultural diversity and eager to address these questions in a creative and constructive way. What he wrote about the relationship of Christianity to other religions applies all the more to its relationship to different cultures:

> To the extent that Christianity opens itself to other traditions, it will become different. Not that it will be less Christian or cease to be Christian altogether. It will simply be taking one more step toward catholicity, the fullness it claims to anticipate in the coming reign of God.

Acknowledgments

When the chair of the Theology Department of Boston College, Professor Catherine Cornille, invited me to give the Duffy Lectures during the academic year 2015–16, I tried to decline on account of prior commitments and scheduling constraints, but her gentle persistence and gracious accommodation of my situation ensured a successful lecture series. My sincere gratitude to her and her colleagues at Boston College, in particular James Keenan, SJ, M. Shawn Copeland, Lisa Sowle Cahill, David Hollenbach, SJ (now at Georgetown University), and Kristin Heyer. During the lectures, the audience was sympathetic and also critical and constructive in their reception of my narrative. I have used their feedback to develop further my narrative. They, too, deserve my thanks and gratitude.

James Keane, formerly Acquisitions Editor at Orbis Books, and Editor-in-Chief and Publisher of Orbis Books, Robert Ellsberg, made sure that I did not renege on my commitment to rework the lectures for publication. But it was my good friend Susan Perry who heroically came out of retirement to guide this book through the editorial process and production. While I take full responsibility for the contents of this book—warts, moles, and all—it was her editorial diligence and dexterity that gave it its final and fitting form. Thank you, Sue!

My Jesuit companions and many collaborators in Africa and Madagascar and beyond remain a constant source of support and encouragement, for which I am deeply grateful. As always, this roll call of gratitude would be incomplete without special mention of my brother, Chuks Afiawari, SJ; my colleague, *Kijana wa Zamani*, Joe Healey, MM; and most of all my dear friend and soulmate, *Oghomwen n'Oghomwen*, Dr. Anne Arabome, SSS. *Asanteni sana!*

Introduction

The African, who becomes a Christian, does not
disown himself or herself.

—*Pope Paul VI*

"Africa," says veteran writer Ben Okri, "breathes stories," and
where I come from we speak in stories and proverbs. Orality
takes precedence over literacy. The internationally acclaimed
Nigerian novelist Chinua Achebe spoke for this culture when
he wrote that words are like yams, and proverbs are the palm
oil with which they are eaten. Narratives in the form of stories, myths, and legends, generously seasoned with proverbs,
formed the staples of my early childhood. An African proverb
resembles a biblical parable in that it modestly aims to teach
a lesson, only pithily. Unlike the biblical parable, however, an
African proverb needs no explanation; it is self-explanatory, it
reveals and imparts its meaning by the sheer force of symbolic
evocation.

The contents of this book were presented originally as the
Duffy Lectures in the Theology Department of Boston College,
Massachusetts, in the United States. But the totality represents
several years of experience and reflection on my multifaceted
religious heritage as a convert to Catholic Christianity from
African Religion. In various instances and on numerous platforms I have developed and expressed aspects of this book to

a variety of audiences. For this publication, I have collected my thoughts and attempted to present them as a consistent narrative to achieve two primary objectives: first, to critique African religious performance and practice in their current public and institutional forms; and, second, to retrieve African Religion as a repository of wisdom and practical insight for the spiritual renewal of all people through its endless quest for meaning, purpose, and wholeness.

To a large extent I have maintained an oral narrative style. In a certain sense, perhaps, this book does not qualify as a typical theological text, but any perceived lack of theological credentials represents the least of my concerns. I want this book to be readable and easily digestible, even when the contents are not readily palatable. The words "study," "analysis," "investigation," "exploration," and "reflection" may appear on several pages of this book. Strictly speaking, though, it is none of these, although perhaps "exploration" or "reflection" comes close. I am trying to tell a story, or rather tell of my religious experience as story. In some instances, I revert to my default mode of theologizing. Such is the extent to which I have strayed over the years from the carefree and uncomplicated milieu of storytelling into the domain of academic and analytical theology. Fortunately I believe the situation is not irreversible. In point of fact, my aim is to undertake a running commentary on faith, religion, and church in Africa today.

My many interlocutors include theologians, historians, and social scientists. But I also probe texts such as official declarations and empirical studies related to faith, religion, and the church in Africa and the world. Unarguably the main source of inspiration for this book is experience—the outcome of all my religious experiences. Long before I could put a precise name on it, religious practice for me has always been a source of fascination and befuddlement in equal measure. Rites, rituals, and worship captivated my imagination, but codes, creeds, and doctrines confounded me. While the former seemed natural, the latter appeared contrived. What is more, it seemed to me that the latter had guardians whose specialty was gauging and maintaining the purity of doctrinal and creedal statements lest they be tainted by irreverent and heretical tendencies. The more I have contended with this puritanical proclivity in my Catholic Christian faith, the stronger the fascination with my African religious imagination has grown. With the passing of time I have come to discover precious gems of this imagination, submerged under the historical and towering edifices of Christianity and Islam.

As I will repeatedly note throughout this book, although Christianity and Islam have claimed victory over African Religion—on the basis of their numerical superiority—such enthusiastic declarations may be premature. African Religion is active in many more ways than most Christian missionaries have taken the time to understand, and it has a lot to teach us on matters of faith, religion, and church.

Two key terms in the subtitle of this book—"confessions" and "animist"—deserve explanation. And I should point out that for me the subtitle is more significant than the rather generic title. Yes, I'm addressing religion and faith in present-day Africa, but from a very particular perspective, thus the subtitle *Confessions of an Animist*. I do not mean "confessions" in the Augustinian sense of a partial autobiography. This book does contain some biographical details, but I try either to keep them to a minimum or to present them in general terms. Nor is "confessions" intended as an account of moral flaws, a crime, or even heroic personal stunts and exploits. To the extent that they exist I reserve those for the confessional.

"Confessions" is my preferred term for stating a personal view and conviction drawn from experience, reflection, and understanding. Thus the confessed views and convictions are personal. In simple terms they are the way I see things in relation to faith, religion, and church in Africa today. This personal viewpoint is further reinforced by a narrative style. However, somewhat akin to Saint Augustine's confessions, which were intended to be read out loud, *Confessions of an Animist* was originally spoken as a series of public lectures. Those who heard it responded with critical comments and questions. I have taken these responses into consideration, and they have contributed immensely in helping me expand my thought, clarify my views, and refine my convictions. Nevertheless, it is important to keep in mind that at the core of these "confessions" are the lived realities that I have attempted to put into words and shape into a story.

As for the second term, "animist," I admit that it conjures up dark and negative images of religious beliefs and practices. As I attempt to demonstrate in this book, it is a label coined by pretenders to a "higher" form of religiosity to denigrate the religious worldview and practices of so-called primitives. In this arrangement, the former created, embellished, and controlled the narrative by which the latter were evaluated, judged, and condemned. An African proverb says that until the lion learns to speak and write, the tale of the hunt will always glorify the hunter. When missionaries, colonials, and anthropologists affixed the label "animist" to the religious practices of the other, in this case practitioners of African Religion, they were playing the hunter. Adopting the term "animist" is in part an act of protest against the injury inflicted on the prey. Also, it is an act of recognition and solidarity with the valuable wisdom and insight of a grossly misunderstood and misrepresented religious tradition.

The term "animist" fulfills a more positive role in this book. A central part of my argument claims that when applied to the religious traditions in Africa, the label "animist" is a distortion of the lived reality. It is based on stereotypes rather than on an objective description of the way of life of the African people. What I call animism is different from what colonial and missionary Christianity meant by the term. As I see it, although heavily dirtied by colonial prejudice and racial bias, animism embodies a profound rootedness in the Spirit that enlivens all things. It is primarily an experience of and capacity for connectedness with the core of every reality. For me, animism is about affirming and reverencing what Pope Francis calls the "divine caress" that vivifies the human and material universe. By claiming and honoring my experience, legacy, and heritage of African Religion, I desire to repudiate any attempt to denigrate its vast repository of meaning; equally important, I hope to generate new insights that yield an expanded understanding of religious experience, both personally and communally.

An overview of this book may be helpful to the reader. In chapter 1 I present a narrative of African Religion on its own terms and note its potential for contributing positive values to human flourishing in Africa. In chapter 2 I acknowledge the historic and stupendous growth of both Christianity and Islam in Africa, but caution against the temptation to assess this growth solely on the strength of numbers and at the expense of the continued relevance of African Religion. Chapter 3 is a sobering account of the claims, contestations, and conflicts that beset religions in Africa, while chapter 4 presents and analyzes ways in which religion is used and abused. Chapter 5 focuses on the pressing issues of ecology and climate change, exploring how African Religion can provide an essential impetus to care for our common home. Chapter 6 extends the argument of chapter 4, but with a particular emphasis on gender rhetoric in the Catholic Church and the irreplaceable and often neglected role of women in church and society in Africa and the wider world. The final chapter is an attempt to peer into the future and anticipate the prospects and directions of religion in Africa.

My main thesis is that religion works in Africa for good and for ill and that understanding its functioning is essential to harnessing and benefiting from its potential. This requires a fresh and critical perception of the symbiotic relationship that exists among the three principal traditions, namely, African Religion, Christianity, and Islam.

My "confessions" constitute indeed a collection of insights from the lived reality of African Religion. I contend that African Religion is no more animistic than certain devotional and sacramental practices of Christianity, which can be superstitious and even idolatrous. My "confessions" contain not the whole truth, but a truth perceived from a personal perspective—a perspective *animated* by the spirituality of African Religion. Absolutism has no place in the kind of religious sensitivity and imagination that I intend this book to explore and expound. If one thing stands, another stands beside it. Or, as an African proverb says, "One person cannot embrace the baobab tree."

I

Faith of My Father,
Spirit of My Mother

The river never flows backward.

—*African proverb*

No matter how many times a leopard crosses a
river, it never loses its spots.

—*African proverb*

There was a time when I was not a Christian. My faith journey
divides into three distinct but overlapping phases. In the beginning, I was born into African Religion and later converted to
Christianity. Christianity taught me a strong disdain for all
things fetishist and animist, for that was how good Christians
were catechized to perceive African Religion. The transition
from African Religion to Christianity was a clean break—or
at least such was the expectation—judging by the vehemence
with which the catechism rejected any traditional religious
practice and all those Africans who in their blindness persisted
in following that way of life.

Fortunately for me, a radical break with a past that was deemed cursed and diabolical never quite materialized. Over time, I have learned to adopt a critical yet respectful and appreciative distance vis-à-vis these two phases of my religious experience. This standpoint of critique, respect, and appreciation constitutes a third distinct phase, and it is driven by a passionate quest to integrate, converge, and harmonize seemingly disparate and conflictual claims and contestations among the religious traditions that dominate the African landscape. The trajectory embedded in these three phases of religious experience explains in part the origin and nature of this book.

Although I begin with an account of the past, this book is not about the past. It is a narrative of an unfolding personal journey that describes present experiences and traces future directions of the workings of religious traditions on a continent pulsating irrepressibly with life and besieged doggedly by death. In his writing Ugandan theologian Emmanuel Katongole portrays both facets of Africa's socioreligious history in imageries of churches and coffins.[1]

Wherever you look in sub-Saharan Africa you see churches. Some of these churches are mobile and follow you wherever you go. I recall countless times when I have boarded public transportation in different African cities, usually a bus, expecting a quiet and hassle-free ride, when without warning a passenger (usually a man) springs from his seat and begins to preach. The concluding rite of this mobile evangelism is even more intriguing as the preacher invariably takes up a collection. The passengers oblige generously and gratefully and no one complains.

In Nairobi where I live there is a slum called Kibera. It is estimated that a million people live on this small patch of land; some claim the number is higher. Whether or not the statistics agree, the reality is that the place is crammed with human beings. Water is scarce in Kibera and so is electricity. Even scarcer are toilets. It is in Kibera that the infamous practice of "flying toilets" was born. Because there are no actual toilets, residents resort to using plastic bags. A typical method of disposal is to fling the bag of waste as far as possible from the owner's immediate locale, hence the name "flying toilet." While toilets are scarce, everywhere you look there are churches. Neither are mosques few and far between. That Kibera has places of worship everywhere but no toilets is now an oft-told joke.

Churches are hardly ever a dull affair on the continent. Visitors to Africa often marvel at and mock in equal measure the vibrancy, chaos, and long hours that characterize lively and lengthy worship celebrations. Fortunately, most often marvel seems to trump mockery. Going to church and participating in worship service is a serious affair. Some services take an entire day, and yet worshipers go home longing for more. The ministers, pastors, evangelists, and preachers come in all stripes. Some are struggling upstarts with worship space no more than a tin shack. But they are hopeful that one day they will make it or, to use the proper religious register, be accorded a divine breakthrough. Those who make it are the "big boys" who count their followers in millions and boast multiple branches across countries and continents.

Consider the example of Nigerian pastor and televangelist Temitope Balogun Joshua who presides as General Overseer of the Synagogue, Church of all Nations (SCOAN). The self-styled prophet's miraculous spectacle is broadcast live across the globe from the dusty enclave of Nigeria's commercial capital of Lagos via his personal television network, Emmanuel TV. "Mega" is the commonly reserved term to describe the sprawling networks of the Christian communities of T. B. Joshua and other African Christian leaders. SCOAN draws multinational visitors in busloads and planeloads, a fact tragically demonstrated when a purpose-built hostel for international guests collapsed in 2014 and crushed 115 worshipers to death. Most of the victims were South Africans, and their death outraged the government of the Republic of South Africa, resulting in a diplomatic spat. Visa restrictions still exist for South Africans wishing to visit Nigeria for religious purposes. While the nationalities of victims were kept as a matter of state secret, the dead faithful were returned in coffins to their respective countries. A few years later, SCOAN, the prophet's evangelical empire, continues to throb with life.

The focus of this first chapter is threefold. First, it offers a personal narrative of experiences that have influenced and formed my consciousness, understanding, and practice of religion. I have referred to this above as the first phase of my religious trajectory. Second, it sketches a portrait of religion and its functioning in Africa, taking into account the second phase of my conversion to Catholic Christianity. And third, it attempts to answer the question of what good can come out of Africa's religious experience. The overall objective is to demonstrate the connectedness of all three issues; although they may appear separate, I consider them interrelated and overlapping.

Africa, My Africa

My first task is to dispel some preconceived notions of life in Africa and to deal with a certain methodological complexity concerning the continent. Africa tends to be known through the bias of stereotypical images and sweeping generalizations as the place of malaria, mosquitoes, Ebola, HIV/AIDS, tropical heat, poverty, hunger, wars, refugees, wildlife, safaris, and so on. Add to that the dozens of iconic portrayals of Africa in Hollywood blockbusters—*Out of Africa*, *The African Queen*, *The Ghost and the Darkness*, *Blood Diamond*, *Hotel Rwanda*, *The Lion King*, *The Gods Must Be Crazy*, and *The Last King of Scotland*, to name a few. In reality, few non-Africans truly know the continent. As Molefi Kete Asante is keen to point out, "At the top of the twentieth century Africa remains the most misunderstood of continents, crippled in our imagination by images rooted in the minds of imperial Europeans who attempted to shape and invent an Africa useful to their political ambitions."[2]

I like poetry. Poems have a way of narrating the complexity of reality in powerful and subtly evocative and vivid terms. While Africa is the subject of many poems, the poem that most captures its historical complexity, at least in my mind, is "Africa, My Africa," by the Senegalese-Cameroonian poet David Mandessi Diop (1927–1960).

Africa, my Africa
Africa of proud warriors in ancestral savannahs
Africa of whom my grandmother sings
On the banks of the distant river
I have never known you
But your blood flows in my veins
Your beautiful black blood that irrigates the fields
The blood of your sweat
The sweat of your work
The work of your slavery
Africa, tell me Africa
Is this you, this back that is bent
This back that breaks
Under the weight of humiliation
This back trembling with red scars
And saying yes to the whip under the midday sun
But a grave voice answers me
Impetuous child that tree, young and strong
That tree over there
Splendidly alone amidst white and faded flowers
That is your Africa springing up anew
Springing up patiently, obstinately
Whose fruit bit by bit acquires
The bitter taste of liberty.

Diop paints a portrait of a painful yet hopeful reality. Pain and hope do abound in Africa, albeit these are oftentimes buried under the debris of colonial history and prejudicial stereotypes. Stereotypes of Africa have a long history. Joseph Conrad called Africa the "Heart of Darkness"; William Whitaker Shreeve baptized it "The White Man's Grave"; Henry Morton Stanley nicknamed it "the Dark Continent"; and *The Economist* magazine branded it "The Hopeless Continent." The nineteenth-century German philosopher Immanuel Kant and his ideological heir Georg W. F. Hegel both indulged in convoluted arguments to prove the anthropological "stupidity" of Africans, whom they termed a pitiable specimen of "the natural man in his completely wild and untamed state"[3] and "the Unhistorical, Undeveloped Spirit, still involved in the conditions of mere nature."[4] Variations and varieties of such unflattering and racially biased perceptions, however and wherever they still exist, constitute idiosyncratic social labels deliberately fabricated to demean and dehumanize a continent of people. The labels are even more vicious when applied to the religious practices of this people.

To attain a meaningful engagement with Africa, it is important to shed the misconception that Africa is a simple entity and to keep in mind the fact that Africa is a complex reality. To learn about Africa first entails a process of unlearning stereotypes, prejudices, and biases. Africa is not one thing. The African narrative is not a single story: it does not consist of one thing, and it means different things to different people. Africa is a million things: fifty-four countries, one billion people (and counting), and up to three thousand languages are compressed into one vast geo-political entity! By any calculation, that qualifies Africa as complex, if not bewildering.

From the point of view of methodology, neither the continent's history nor its identity can be facilely summarized or explained. South African columnist Sandile Memela sums up this methodological complexity rather perceptively:

I don't know if there is any single person who has authority and power to tell us what constitutes Africanness. But even if this elusive and essential African identity exists, it cannot be something static. It is dynamic, forward-moving, and undergoing constant change and transformation. This Africanness has not only connected the cultural preservationists who want to freeze culture into an unchanging pre-colonial mode, but integrates progressives who want to push its boundaries to the limits of postmodernism to absorb global influences and their elements. And this Africanness is not about the amount of melanin in your skin.[5]

Assessing Africa has never been easy. It is a zone of ardent contestation between preservationists and progressives. When it comes to understanding, portraying, or narrating Africa, Africans can always protest by a simple "that's not *my* Africa!" Nonetheless, without exception or hesitation everyone can proclaim with former South African president Thabo Mbeki, "I am an African. I owe my being to the hills and the valleys, the mountains and the glades, the rivers, the deserts, the trees, the flowers, the seas and the ever-changing seasons that define the face of our native land."[6]

The Africa I am describing here is a snapshot of a few short strands drawn from the multifaceted tapestry of all Africa. It is my view as an African of the place and the role of faith and religion on this continent. Despite my penchant to speak and write freely of Africa and Africans, I do not possess an understanding of the continent as a whole. I came from one ethnic group in one country, and today I live and work among several ethnic groups in a different country. Yet an African proverb counsels that to eat an elephant you start piece by piece, which is a useful attitude for any methodology.

The Medicine Room

I grew up knowing my father and mother as adherents and practitioners of a spiritual way of life. Life meant something more to them than what was immediately visible and tangible. Or, to put it differently, every single reality seemed imbued with a purpose, a sense, and a meaning. Nothing was superfluous, useless, or unimportant. And most things were reusable and recyclable.

The most important part of the house where I grew up was the "medicine room." This small, dark enclosure was curtained with strips of fresh palm fronds and crowded with figurines, statuettes, and altars dedicated to a phalanx of gods and goddesses. Besides serving as a domestic pantheon, the room housed an assortment of large, deep clay pots perpetually bubbling with a hodgepodge of aromatic herbal concoctions, alongside a collection of ancestral staffs, each one carefully positioned on an angle against the wall, symbolizing a founding ancestor of the family's lineage. To be in proximity to the medicine room occasioned an eerie feeling of religious dread. One never entered uninvited or uninitiated. As a child I viewed the medicine room as a zone of concentrated spiritual energy. It served as the center and focus of worship for our extended family, and thus it generated fascination, dread, and spiritual renewal in equal measure. Oftentimes, my father would disappear into the medicine room, and when he reemerged his countenance glowed with the confidence and awe of one who had glimpsed an aspect of divinity. Whatever he did inside that room transformed him; we could see the surge in confidence and his increased zest for life.

Now and then we would be allowed to draw water from the ancestral clay pots mounted in the medicine room. No one knew how old those clay pots were, much less the chemistry of their contents. Judging by their pungent aroma and their pale-dark coloration, we assumed the origins of the clay pots and perhaps their liquid content stretched back several generations. The liquids seemed to be brewed to the same degree of spiritual concentration and energy that pervaded and radiated from the room and we knew that the water from the clay pots was very potent. We believed in its ability to fortify our spirits, sanctify our enterprises, and ward off enemy-instigated evil attacks on our bodies and homestead. The prescription for this ritual spiritual and corporal fortification called for a bowlful or more mixed with bath water for our periodic ablutions. The effect was instantaneous, or at least so we believed. The waters perfumed our bodies like no other fragrance did; we smelled of the spirits of our ancestors.

My mother was a devotee of the goddess of the sea, *Olokun*, the giver of prosperity and fertility. She too had her shrine and an assortment of bleached clay figurines adorning the altar to her goddess. It is a common practice for devotees to place items of value on the altar of *Olokun*—chinaware, ivory carvings, brass plates, and bronze ornaments.

As an aside, perhaps the most painful assault of missionaries on this way of life happened when a devotee of this goddess was converted to Christianity. Usually the missionary would collect all the items from the altar for destruction and disposal. However, there are some who now claim that such objects of value were routinely shipped overseas to adorn mission offices and museums.

Back to my mother's goddess. As often as my mother would consult with her goddess, surrounded mostly by other women devotees, she would be possessed by her spirit and thus be renewed and revived. To invite the spirit of her goddess to possess her, she would dance with a small clay pot on her head. As her steps quickened and her gyrations intensified, her countenance was transformed and she became one with the spirit of her goddess. To a child watching from the safe distance of the corner of the room, there was enough power, energy, and vitality on display to capture the imagination and to shape a religious consciousness. Making sense of it all was not an immediate or important preoccupation. It sufficed to be present and watch, riveted and enraptured.

My father did something else that rattled my imagination. In addition to the regular rhythm of ritual worship, he took time to entreat another god. Very early in the morning, long before everybody else could shake off the slumber of the night and the rising sun set aglow the surface of nature, he would kneel down and with both elbows planted firmly on his bed present a series of entreaties to an invisible deity. The addressee was *Osanobua*. Unlike the other gods and goddesses of the medicine room and the side altars, the praise names for *Osanobua* were strikingly different and unique. *Osanobua* was the creator of human beings and the universe, the strong arm that makes possible the impossible, the sustainer of the universe, the unbreakable stone, and the owner of our heads.

Judging by the litany of attributes reserved for *Osanobua*, this god did not share divinity or supremacy with any other god. There was no material representation of this god in the same way that the gods and goddesses of the medicine room and side altars were depicted. Who was *Osanobua*? Whenever I was privileged to witness and participate in my father's dawn ritual of supplication, the ending caught my attention: my father's tone of voice was greatly amplified when he concluded "in the name of the only begotten son, *Ijesu Kristi,* who sets us free."

The relationship between *Osanobua, Ijesu Kristi, Olokun, Ogun, Isango, Orumila,* and the pantheon of divinities and deities to which I was exposed defied comprehension. Yet the adults seemed to navigate this maze of religious transactions effortlessly. They were oblivious of the haze gathering and settling on the imagination of a child who had neither the capacity nor the means to process or make sense of this religious spectacle.

Partial comprehension and understanding would come later on when I read Chinua Achebe's *Things Fall Apart*. Although I doubt that the author's primary intention was to settle the religious inquiries of a befuddled teenager, his literary account touched on numerous religious themes, one of them being the relationship between the categories of divinities and deities. I read his account before I converted to Catholic Christianity. And it made eminent sense to me. I still remember one particularly interesting scenario of a theological conversation between a Christian missionary and a practitioner of African Religion, the former intent on converting the latter to his religious views:

> Whenever Mr. Brown went to that village he spent long hours with Akunna in his *obi* (hut) talking through an interpreter about religion. Neither of them succeeded in converting the other but they learned more about their different beliefs.
>
> "You say that there is one supreme God who made heaven and earth," said Akunna on one of Mr. Brown's visits. "We also believe in Him and call Him Chukwu. He made all the world and the other gods."
>
> "There are no other gods," said Mr. Brown. "Chukwu is the only God and all others are false. You can carve a piece of wood—like that one" (he pointed at the rafters from which Akunna's carved *Ikenga* [ancestral staff] hung), "and you call it a god. But it is still a piece of wood."
>
> "Yes," said Akunna. "It is indeed a piece of wood. The tree from which it came was made by Chukwu, as indeed all minor gods were. But He made them for His messengers so that we could approach Him through them. . . ."[7]

Chief Akunna's theological astuteness shone through in this intriguing conversation. Although his unrelenting interlocutor mustered ad hominem arguments against the chief's position, he held his ground:

"[Chukwu] appoints the smaller gods to help Him because His work is too great for one person. . . .

"We make sacrifices to the little gods, but when they fail and there is no one else to turn to we go to Chukwu. It is right to do so. We approach a great man through his servants. But when his servants fail to help us, then we go to the last source of hope. We appear to pay greater attention to the little gods but that is not so. We worry them more because we are afraid to worry their Master. Our fathers knew that Chukwu was the Overlord and that is why many of them gave their children the name Chukwuka—'Chukwu is Supreme.'"[8]

Like Chief Akunna, in the normal course of daily living both my father and my mother regularly performed rituals to their coterie of gods and goddesses, rituals in which the entire extended family and sometimes the neighborhood participated. Food was offered and a libation was poured generously to propitiate the spirits of the ancestors and mother earth. But when they named their children it was in honor of *Osanobua*, the Supreme Being, the author of life and the creator of the universe. Hence, among my many names, I also answer to *Osa-hon-erhumwun-mwen*—"*Osanobua* heard my prayer."

In all of these moments, as a child I was a curious onlooker, mystified, perplexed, and enthralled by the intercourse of human beings and the spirits. None of the principal participants was a sophisticated theologian; participation didn't require religious artistry and formulaic mastery of rubrics or doctrines. It sufficed to present oneself, and the encounter happened there and then. Although I did not realize it as a child, over time I have come to believe that I am the progeny of a priest and a priestess. This realization has a bearing on all three phases of my unfolding spiritual pilgrimage and theological quest.

Inside the Mind of an Animist

The scenario that I have described above may seem bizarre to some readers, resembling at best a scene from *Harry Potter*, or, at worst, a clip from the witch-hunt movie *The Crucible*. Yet these experiences were my earliest exposure to the meaning and practice of religion, and they influenced and formed my religious perception, imagination, and consciousness. Curiously, however, my father and my mother would have been utterly nonplussed at the question "What is your religion?" They did not use the term "religion" to describe their experience and practice. For them, what they did was simply *our way of life*. This life originated from and unfolded in a spiritual *ethnosphere*. It was sustained by an unwritten code and practice that had been handed down by another generation, embodied in mystery and spirituality, rooted in transcendence and immanence, and expressed through ritual and worship, myths and narratives, ethics and norms.

As the scholar of religion Benjamin C. Ray has correctly noted, "The word religion is a late-comer to the scholarly discourse about Africa, and is still noticeably absent in most popular descriptions of African cultures."[9] However, when colonial missionaries, contemporary scholars, and commentators discuss "African Traditional Religion," they equate it with animism. Typically the classification partitions Africa among Islam, Christianity, and animism.

The term "animism" never ceases to intrigue me. I believe that a close study of it would yield a wealth of insight on spirituality as I experienced it and as it continues to influence my religious imagination and practice. As I attempt to demonstrate later in chapter 5, a correct understanding of the dynamics of animism is helpful in exploring the transformative dimensions of human and physical ecology in our age of global warming and climate change.

As an anthropological construct, "animism" covers a broad spectrum of religious beliefs, attitudes, and practices whose common denominator is the investment of natural objects with power, energy, or vitality. Very simply it is a "belief in spirits" embodied in nature. For some scholars of religion, it is understood to belong to one of the earliest stages in the evolutionary trajectory of religion and the lowest possible rung in the ladder of religious consciousness. In this classification, "animist" exemplifies the polar opposite of "superior." Such a colonial taxonomy of religion hardens "animism" into a normative definition of primitive and inferior religious beliefs and practices, thus giving animism a long litany of synonyms that include "fetishism, idolatry, superstition, heathenism, totemism, magic. . . ."[10]

During the advent of missionary Christianity, especially in the nineteenth century, this derogatory classification of African religious traditions had two pernicious consequences. First, it meant that Africans did not in fact have a religion. At best, whatever ritual actions Africans performed were pale approximations of religion; at worst, they were animist and fetishist. Second, as a result of the first point, early European missionaries justified their aggressive attempts to eradicate superstition, magic, paganism, and fetishism in Africa and to foist a new religion on Africans.[11]

As Benjamin Ray points out, the term "religion" was a late comer in Africa, and several indigenous African languages still do not use the word "religion" to describe what Africans believe and what they practice. Ugandan poet Okot p'Bitek has noted that "the concepts of 'fetishism' or 'animism' . . . were not African religions. . . . There is no such religion as animism in Africa."[12] In this sense, African Religion construed or defined as "animism" is an exonym—a term used by an outsider (in this case Christian missionaries) to describe another group of people. While the missionaries were quite content to refer to Africans using this term, the latter were not. There is nothing wrong with the use of exonyms; indeed, they are a common feature of socio-linguistic and geographical significations. To foreigners, Firenze is Florence, Deutsch is German, and Masr is Egypt. But unlike typical exonyms, there is no correspondence or equivalence between what foreigners label "animism" and what Africans believe and practice.

In my experience, African religious traditions represent an all-encompassing framework of meaning and practice that regulates political governance, economic transactions, and social interactions. They offer a set of values and norms that shape socio-political behavior within a context in which all the people subscribe to certain moral codes, underpinned by belief in spirits, deities, gods, goddesses, and ancestors. Within this framework, diviners, herbalists, priests, priestesses, and numerous specialists play a vital role as overseers of socio-political and moral rectitude in contexts where, because of shared tenets and beliefs, spiritual practice appears to intersect with life in a harmonious and unobtrusive manner.

As an African child growing up in the ancient city of Benin in southern Nigeria, I, too, would have been categorized as "animist," along with my father, my mother, and my entire family, albeit the more common practice at the time for Christians was to label us as "pagans" or "heathens." A personal anecdote demonstrates this deprecatory stereotypical labeling.

My mother was born in 1939 in the heyday of British colonialism and European missionary Christianity in the fairly recently created nation of Nigeria. At sixteen, the same age at which I converted to Christianity, she was baptized. Her Certificate of Baptism shows that the baptism took place in the Parish of Christ Church Onitsha in the Diocese of the Niger, Christmas Eve, in 1957. Under the column "Former Religion in case of Adults," the Reverend Canon Ezekwesili ("By whom the Ceremony was performed") entered "Heathenism." It was to this heathen that I was born ten years later.

Animism Embodied

As should be clear by now, "animism" has been and still is a pejorative and derogatory label. In past and present times it has accorded social scientists, historians, and theologians a useful tool for signifying and codifying the religion of the other, in this case African Religion. Evidence demonstrates that this exercise of signification and codification portrays its referent as primitive and heathen. Little doubt exists in my mind that this approach is irrational and reductionist. It characteristically simplifies a very complex reality. However, by accepting the label "animist" I wish to advance a narrative and evaluate African religious experience based on a firsthand encounter rather than on stereotypes and prejudices. I am deeply concerned about a critical but respectful appreciation of the values inherent in African Religion while simultaneously remaining committed to the tenets of the gospel as the primary repository of the Christian message.

What is it really like to be an animist? In responding to this question, my principal aim is to outline the foundations of a religious imagination, practice, and consciousness routinely disparaged by adherents of the so-called world religions. From my recollection, and as I continue to draw inspiration from this tradition, central to the whole religious system throughout Africa is a *deep belief in the livingness of creation*. In other words, this tradition represents a profound and intense belief that nothing is lifeless in my natural surroundings, and that "there is inner invisible power in anything at any given moment."[13] Transposed in the words of Pope Francis in his encyclical, *Laudato Si': On Care for Our Common Home*, this means "that each creature has its own purpose. None is superfluous. . . . Soil, water, mountains: everything is, as it were, a caress of God" (*LS* 84).

From the ancestral tree, *Ikhinmwin* (*Newbouldia laevis*) that stood at the center of the homestead,[14] to the river that flowed eastward of the city, and the whirlwind that we believed often whisked people off to the world of spirits, everything in the immediate natural environment of my religious upbringing exuded power, energy, and vitality. There was hardly a thing that did not command some measure of respect, each with its own purpose. The ancestral tree was an object of reverence, and it marked the sacred space and place of worship and ritual performances for our homestead. Nobel laureate Wangari Maathai confirms this belief when she states that trees like this one are "understood by their communities as nodal points that connect the world above with the world below . . . places where one's ancestors and/or their spirits reside."[15] That was how we understood and related to the ever-green *Ikhinmwin*.

A medicine room is not simply a room in a house, a tree is not just a tree. Little wonder then that, besides connecting two worlds, it provides a space of gathering and communion for families and communities where differences are settled and vital connections and relationships are reestablished. Its importance resides in part in the manner in which it facilitates the vital relationality of the vertical and the horizontal dimensions of existence.

The river also commanded deference; it was the object of veneration for devotees of the water goddess. The whirlwind instilled religious awe. No ordinary wind, it was the instrument of the gods. When later I learned about the doctrine of creation in Christianity and the sacramentality present in Catholicism, it made sense to think of the "wind," "breath," or "spirit" of God hovering over the waters, caressing the universe, and quickening nature into life at the dawn of creation (Genesis 1:1). And my understanding of "dominion over all the creatures of the earth" (Gen 1:28) draws significance from this religious upbringing.

As a convert to Catholic Christianity, like millions of other Africans I have made the transition from my ancestral faith to the Christian faith. This is not an easy transition to make or to navigate. It would be pretentious to claim that I have made a clean break with my past; I think this is probably impossible. The present is always imbued with the past; hence my predilection for terms like journey, path, trajectory, and pilgrimage when describing my religious experience. Perhaps it would have been easier to sever the bond to that past if it consisted solely in replaceable creeds, doctrines, and dogmas. On the contrary, it was and it remains *a way of life*. And to quote an African proverb, "No matter how many times a leopard crosses a river, it never loses its spots." I have resisted and I continue to resist the notion that my African way of life, rooted in the faith of my father and animated by the spirit of my mother, amounts to no more than an irrational quest for God in "shadows and images"—to use another derogatory phrase from Vatican II's *Lumen Gentium* (Dogmatic Constitution on the Church, 16). The way of life of my parents relied on images to facilitate the encounter with a luminous and tangible realm of mystery; it radiated energy and evoked mystery and respect rather than shadows.

Likewise, I do not perceive myself as torn between two religious traditions. Neither do I accept the label of "faith schizophrenia" or "religious double-mindedness" that some theologians routinely foist on Africans who believe that God continues to speak through their ancestral way of life even as God reveals God's self in Jesus Christ. This is an experience of tension rather than division, of inspiration rather than despair. It is a quest for integration and harmony rather than an experience of alienation and conflict. For this reason, I derive immense solace from the counsel of Pope Paul VI (1897–1978) who said that "the African, who becomes a Christian, does not disown himself [or herself], but takes up the age-old values of tradition 'in spirit and in truth.'"[16]

I do not pretend to imply that African Religion is a pristine oasis of ethical purity. Rather, I feel that labeling it what it is not distorts and discounts the religious experience of millions of people. Instead, my claim is that African Religion, a vital religious experience and spiritual imagination still active in many parts of Africa, possesses a real genius capable of renewing the global community of believers.

Some Guiding Instructions for the Road

Africa is a deeply religious continent. In subsequent chapters I will reference empirical data showing unprecedented and sustained growth in religious affiliation in Africa. In light of this phenomenon, it is important to understand some underlying factors that have led to these present developments.

I hasten to add that religious growth represents only one dimension of the current socioeconomic and political situation of Africa. There are other important issues that I will discuss in the course of this narrative. I focus primarily on the religious experience because of the way it intersects with the other dimensions of life in Africa. Part of the power and fascination of African Religion lies in its capacity to hold the various challenges of life in healthy tension, while simultaneously giving its adherents the ability to cope and function reasonably well.

A first explanation for the exponential growth of Christianity and Islam on the continent lies deep in the anthropological constitution of Africans. The African is a believer. The African's experience of faith did not begin with the advent of missionaries—Christian or Muslim. My own experience of growing up in a traditional household is testament to this assertion. In the context of Africans' religious imagination and consciousness, faith and belief represent an openness to the realm of spiritual reality, one that is immediately accessible in human existence and in nature. It is not, as in the case of some religions, a belief codified in tightly controlled religious systems, practices, or doctrines. I believe this anthropological constitution that is so characteristic of Africans can illumine a path of renewal for the world church.

Pertinent to this conviction is the insight of Pope Emeritus Benedict XVI that Africa "constitutes an immense spiritual 'lung' for a humanity that appears to be in a crisis of faith and hope."[17] This flattering designation expresses an explicit belief in the capability of the religious and spiritual traditions of Africa to resuscitate a spiritually asphyxiated humanity. The incontrovertible evidence of religious growth and spiritual depth in Africa, as interpreted by Benedict XVI, represents a sign of hope for the rest of the world. Africa holds a significant piece of the future of Christianity, or we could say that the future of Christianity passes through Africa. Because numbers alone do not and cannot tell the full story, I hope my narrative expands the scope of this story of religious growth and helps develop a theological evaluation that is both critical and objective.

Second, it is important to remember that the contemporary religious identity of Africa filters through a triple heritage. The African religious framework comprises a trinity of faith traditions: African Religion, Christianity, and Islam. To the chagrin of religious experts, professional theologians, seasoned evangelists, and ecclesiastical authorities, in various parts of the continent people seem at ease with and perfectly capable of mixing and matching elements of these faith traditions. The faith and beliefs of my father are examples of this unconscious blending. This syncretistic proclivity can be interpreted positively as a healthy form of religious coexistence and tolerance, and thus can serve as a resource for the rest of the world. It is a sharp contrast to this era of violent and destructive theological and religious fundamentalism, sectarianism, and extremism. Notwithstanding this positive interpretation, we cannot dismiss the reality of multiple layers of tension among these religious traditions in Africa; examples are not hard to find in the past and present crises in Nigeria, Ivory Coast, Central African Republic, Egypt, Tanzania, Kenya, Mali, Somalia, and several other African countries. They pose a serious challenge to the task of interreligious dialogue and ecumenism. However, I remain unshakeable in my conviction that the unique spirit of hospitality and tolerance that imbues African spirituality can be a resource for global Christianity, which is in need of models of dialogue, tolerance, and mutuality. The present world of religious pluralism and diversity demands peaceful coexistence.

Third, it is well established today that Christianity's center of gravity is shifting dramatically from the global North to the global South, that is, from Europe and North America to Africa, Asia, and Latin America. As a religion moves and shifts geographically, so it changes through encounters with other religions. While I focus here on Christianity, the African traditions of spirituality contain a number of values and characteristics that can contribute to the renewal of global Christianity and global Islam. These include a deep consciousness of transcendence in ordinary, day-to-day living, an attitude of reverence toward human and natural ecologies, a spiritual sense of community, an understanding of life that is expansive and inclusive, a sense of joy in the faith that the people of God profess, a holistic understanding of creation, and a shared responsibility of stewardship for the universe. If, on account of these characteristics and practices, this tradition receives a negative labeling—that of "animist," I am not ashamed to be its proponent. African Religion has molded my religious imagination and continues to positively influence my Christian faith and practice.

It is worth repeating that this brief sketch is not intended to imply that African Religion delineates a haven of bliss and harmony. If anything, a fictional "exoticization" of Africa must be avoided. It is also important to ask whether the portrait painted here of religion in Africa adequately responds to the critique generated by secularism against the adverse effects of religion in a postmodernist era. I do not pretend that religion is innocent of the trials and tribulations of the continent of Africa. In Africa, as elsewhere, religion has been and continues to be used and abused in a variety of ways, some of which I will discuss later on. In making this point I am focusing on the *agency* of adherents rather than on the inherent values and tenets of the religious traditions in Africa. This is an important distinction that should be kept in mind throughout.

Leaving aside these questions for a later discussion, I remain convinced that African spirituality or way of life continues to influence—even if at times imperceptibly—the practice and expression of faith on the continent. I have experienced it up close and personal and learned to understand, respect, critique, and appreciate its values and practices. The faith of my father and the spirit of my mother constitute enduring testaments to the values and resources of African Religion for the renewal of faith, religion, and church in Africa and beyond.

In the final analysis, like the river that never flows backward, I do not anticipate an uncomplicated return to the initial two phases of my religious peregrination. Yet, like the leopard's spots, their imprint on my religious consciousness and theological frame of mind remains indelible. I must carefully negotiate the intersection of the three phases of my religious journey in order to determine its present and future trajectory.

Notes

1. Emmanuel Katongole, *The Sacrifice of Africa: A Political Theology for Africa* (Grand Rapids, MI: Eerdmanns, 2011), 29–32.

2. Daniel M. Mengara, ed., *Images of Africa: Stereotypes and Realities* (Trenton, NJ: Africa World Press, 2001), xiii.

3. G. W. F. Hegel, *The Philosophy of History* (New York: Dover, 1956), 93; see Immanuel Kant, *Observations on the Feeling of the Beautiful and the Sublime* (1764).

4. Hegel, *The Philosophy of History*, 99.

5. http://www.news24.com/Archives/City-Press/The-new-Africanness-20150429.

6. https://www.dkut.ac.ke/downloads/Thabo%20Mbeki_Iam%20an%20African-%20Speech.pdf.

7. Chinua Achebe, *Things Fall Apart* (New York: Doubleday, 1994), 179.

8. Ibid, 180.

9. Benjamin C. Ray, *African Religions: Symbol, Ritual, and Community* (Upper Saddle River, NJ: Pearson, 2000), xi.

10. Ibid.

11. See Laurenti Magesa, *African Religion: The Moral Traditions of Abundant Life* (Maryknoll, NY: Orbis Books, 1997), 14 ff.

12. Quoted in Ray, *African Religions*, xi.

13. Laurenti Magesa, *What Is Not Sacred? African Spirituality* (Maryknoll, NY: Orbis Books, 2013), 27.

14. This was the most important tree in the homestead: "Newbouldia laevis . . . is a tropical plant belonging to the family of *Bignoniaceae*. It is among the most useful plants in Africa and grows up to 10 m in height with a cauliflorous habit. It is an evergreenish plant with a height of approximately 7–8 m high in West Africa and up to 20 m in Nigeria. The plant has characteristic shiny dark green leaves with large purple flowers. Different African countries have different names for Newbouldia laevis, e.g. Togo call it *lifui*, Ghana call it *sesemasa*, Hausa call it *Aduruku*, Igbo call it *ogilisi* or *ògírìsì*, Senegal call it *gimgid*, the Gambia call it *kallihi*, Yoruba call it *Akoko*, Guinea call it *canhom*, Urhobo call it *Ogiriki*, Sierra Leone call it *Sherbro*, Mali call it *kinkin*, Edo state call it *íkhímì*, Tiv call it *Kontor*, while the Ibibio call it *itömö*. Newbouldia laevis has different symbols and meanings to different countries. . . . Some villages in Ivory Coast and Gabon plant the tree near the tombs to act as a protective talisman. The Ibibio and Efik people of Nigeria regard the tree as a symbol of their deities, thus they tend to place it in sacred places. The Igbo part of Nigeria refers to the Newbouldia laevis . . . tree as a sacred tree; thus they usually plant it in front of a chief's house." See https://globalfoodbook.com/incredible-benefits-of-newbouldia-laevis-ogilisi.

15. Wangari Maathai, *Replenishing the Earth: Spiritual Values for Healing Ourselves and the World* (New York: Doubleday, 2010), 93.

16. Paul VI, *Africae Terrarum* (Message to the Countries of Africa, 1967), no. 14.

17. http://www.vatican.va/holy_father/benedict_xvi/homilies/2009/documents/hf_ben-xvi_hom_20091004_sinodo-africa_en.html.

2

The Miracle of a Century

Quidquid recipitur ad modum recipientis recipitur (What is received is received according to the mode of the receiver).

—*Thomas Aquinas*

The astronomical growth of Christianity in sub-Saharan Africa qualifies as an evangelical and statistical miracle. While the numbers may not tell the whole truth, the numbers don't lie. In one of the most extensive surveys ever to be conducted on the growth of religions in Africa, the Pew Forum on Religion and Public Life revealed that one in five of all the Christians in the world, approximately 21 percent, now lives in sub-Saharan Africa. Differently put, in a relatively short period of one hundred years (1910–2010), Christianity in sub-Saharan Africa recorded a nearly seventy-fold increase in membership, from 7 million to 470 million. The methods of computation of such statistics may vary, but they converge on the same conclusion: Christianity is on the rise in Africa, and it does not appear to show any sign of waning.

The data is particularly comforting for the Roman Catholic Church. Georgetown University's Center for Applied Research in the Apostolate (CARA) has observed that, judging by all statistical variables, besides Asia Africa records the most significant growth in the Roman Catholic Church. The number of Catholics in Africa has increased at the phenomenal rate of 238 percent since 1980. Growth in the Catholic population accounts for 23 percent of all population growth in Africa since 1980. The percentage of the African population that is Catholic has increased from 12.5 percent in 1980 to 18.6 percent in 2012.[1]

Further indicators of growth in the Catholic population are evident in the fact that the number of parishes has doubled since 1980. Likewise there is a significant increase in the number of priests in Africa (adding 22,787 priests for a 131 percent increase) and in Asia (adding 32,906 priests for a 121 percent increase) between 1980 and 2012. It is important to note that Africa is not the sole beneficiary of this growth. The CARA study also highlights the growing phenomenon within the Catholic Church of using African and Asian priests in the United States, Europe, and other places where there are too few native priests to staff parishes. This phenomenon of "reverse evangelization" allows Africans and Asians to do to Europe what Europeans did to them, namely, reconvert and convert Europeans to Christianity.

While numbers don't lie, they don't yield much information if they are detached from lived reality. The tale they tell of the unparalleled advance of Christianity takes shape in the throngs of worshipers milling around worship places. Massive or "mega" capacity churches spring up in cities and towns to accommodate the ever-expanding flock of believers. Building a megachurch represents a status symbol that separates accomplished celebrity idols and peers from the upstart preachers and evangelists.

The primary purpose of this chapter is to reflect on this phenomenon of Christianity's growth in sub-Saharan Africa through the eyes of a convert. In the previous chapter I mentioned my transition from African Religion to Christianity. The actual event was nothing spectacular in the face of biblical experiences like the calling of Matthew (Matthew 9:9-13) or Saul's encounter on the road to Damascus (Acts 9:1-19). Mine was less dramatic but quite intentional. In hindsight, it seems to have been an outcome of my inquisitive and impressionable religious imagination and my fascination with religious rites and rituals. Once I resolved to embrace the Christian faith, I committed to a mandatory process of instruction in the faith, which at the time involved a two-year catechetical formation, leading to my formal reception into the Catholic Church. It is critically important for the reader to remind himself or herself that mine is the voice of a convert whose religious imagination has been shaped deeply by the influences of African Religion. This caveat is necessary to set this reflection in its proper context.

This reflection doubles as an exploration of themes in faith, religion, and church in Africa. "Exploration" is preferred to "study" quite simply to preclude the misconception that I am dissecting a static, monolithic, and closed entity. As I have already noted, Africa is not a single story. Woven into the narrative of this book is my conviction that Christianity in Africa is an evolving, even mutating, and complex phenomenon that is not restricted by the usual tools of academic analysis. I view this as positive. There is another side though, which is less complimentary, that exists because of many perceptible inconsistencies between the practice of Christianity as the channel of a radically transformative religious experience and its performance as a superficial, alienating, and ambiguous myth. This negative aspect at best resembles an ambiguous adventure, and at worst a dangerous tool of manipulation in the hands of evangelical charlatans and moguls. This reality is the focus of the following two chapters.

Fully understanding the complexities and ambiguities of Christianity in Africa within the wider context of global Christianity requires taking a fresh look at its history. When the history of Christianity in Africa is viewed not as a succession of past, disjointed events but as an evolution of multiple strands, the intersection and divergence of these strands reveal somewhat perplexing but observable patterns. From its inception, Christianity in Africa has always been bound to global events and developments in history, and only within this global context can we accurately assess its promises and unmask its myths. Accordingly, whatever conclusions we draw will only be valid for a limited period of time, as the reality under consideration continues to move, shift, and mutate with fascinating unpredictability.

Because of this unpredictability, I am adopting a stance of provisionality. My aim is not to close a debate but to advance a conversation. How should we understand Christianity in twenty-first-century Africa? This reflection or exploration must be a work in progress. And progress will come about via the critical contribution of multiple strands of conversation, dialogue, and debate. In formulating and articulating my "take" on Christianity in Africa, I make no pretense at completeness: intellectual modesty demands an admission that the object of this inquiry is too wide in scope and depth for anything approaching a comprehensive account. The origin and rationale of my perspective should be clear by now in the hues and shades that refract through an experience of life and a formative practice of African Religion.

I perceive a major challenge in this undertaking: in one word, the challenge is "Africa." It is, perhaps, a misnomer to speak of "African" Christianity, for the trajectory of Christianity in Africa appears as an amalgam of histories, events, processes, places, and personalities that can hardly be regrouped under one category without committing the egregious twin errors of generalization and simplification. I recognize this as a necessary evil; resistance would be futile.

What accounts for this conundrum? In his characteristic critique of colonial impositions on the continent, Congolese philosopher V. Y. Mudimbe offers a plausible explanation:

"Africa" is an epistemological invention, largely credited to biased and oftentimes distorted Western scholarship. Notwithstanding Mudimbe's stance, "Africa" is an invention that works. Its existence and reality are not in doubt and trying to undo accumulated strata of decadent colonial legacies is a dead end for those in search of the "real" Africa. However we choose to construct it, the collective "Africa" serves as a useful tool. It allows us to analyze situations, assess possibilities, form opinions, follow trends, and generate consensus concerning its reality and existence. It is a recognizable demographic, cultural, socioeconomic, political, and historical entity. History is the dominant focus of this chapter, but its focus is about looking back to see more clearly how we got where we are. But I will tell this history as story.

So, Once upon a Time. . . .

In 1958, a group of Christians of colonial Northern Rhodesia in south central Africa rejoiced in the divinely purposed origin of Christianity in Africa in the following terms: "When Jesus was persecuted by the European Herod, God sent him to Africa; by this we know that Africans have naturally a true spirit of Christianity."[2] In my religious imagination, there is a legitimate justification for the conjunction of "Christianity" and "Africa." But that is hardly a sufficient pretext to make an epistemological jump to the co-naturality of "Africans" and the "true spirit of Christianity." Without any intent of irreverence on my part, for all his widely acclaimed visionary prowess and apocryphal acumen, the Galilean Jewish rabbi Jesus, who practiced his prophetic trade, traversing the wind-swept alleys of Nazareth and, further, the plains of Jewish Palestine, could not have foreseen the phenomenon of Christianity's institution and exponential growth in Africa.

Various myths of origins, like the one attributed to Christians in Northern Rhodesia, claim to pinpoint the historical origin of Christianity somewhere in Africa. The fabled flight of the Holy Family to Egypt is one such myth. An olive tree, one myth goes, that the teenage Jesus planted in Egypt during his days of exile has survived to this day. Tantalizing as they may seem, none of the many versions of this tradition provides the basis for a chronological account of the origins of Christianity in Africa. Despite its biblical foundation, no historical proof exists of the flight of the Holy Family to Egypt or of its decisive role in the institution of Christianity in Africa. To think of Jesus of Nazareth as the historical founder of Christianity in Africa amounts to a facile historicization of mythology. Some stories we simply want to believe. Much of what Christianity's origins in antiquity allow us to affirm is as simple as the beginning of an African tale: "Once upon a time, Christianity came to Africa." No more, no less.

Myths die hard. Although it is easy for twenty-first-century global citizens to dismiss the myth of Jesus' flight to Egypt, including evidence of the putative olive tree, several elements of religious myth-making regarding the origins of Christianity in Africa resiliently adorn the pages of history. I take note of them not as starting points, but as one of many factors that shape our religious imagination and facilitate an understanding of the history and evolution of Christianity in Africa. In other words, myths and traditions allow us to narrate the progress of Christianity as an ongoing story up to where Christianity has reached in Africa today.

The Apostle and the Queen

At the origin of two of the oldest Judeo-Christian traditions in Africa are two legends: the one of an apostle, the other of a queen. By definition a legend is neither historically provable nor objectively verifiable. It is a past that is invented, but never entirely past. Yet it exercises such power on those who adhere to and transmit it as a matter of religious conviction that many an institution has survived for centuries tethered on the flimsiest thread of legends. The stories of the foundation of the Coptic Orthodox Church in Egypt and the Ethiopian Orthodox Tewahido Church in Ethiopia offer fitting examples. The Coptic Orthodox Church claims the evangelist Mark as its founder. With his credentials as the author of a canonical gospel, Mark remains the solid foundation of this isolated enclave of Christian practice surrounded by a vast population of Muslims. On account of its particular history and geographical location, the remnant community of the Church of St. Mark has lived its fragile and contained existence within the boundaries of Egypt, although in times past, for a brief period, it succeeded in making significant forays southward in the direction of the kingdom of Aksum in present-day Ethiopia.

To say that the foundation of the Coptic Orthodox Church is legendary is not to discount the historically proven glories of Christianity in North Africa. Numerous accounts of the colorful personalities (Anthony, Pachomius, Theodore, Athanasius, and so on), momentous events, and exotic sites that characterized Christian North Africa have survived. They are firmly etched in Christian theological traditions and writ large on the map of global Christianity.

Historical records concur that in the first six hundred years of the Common Era, Christian North Africa bustled with religious ferment: there was a flourishing of desert monasticism, the development of theological scholarship, the proliferation of churches, and the presence of fierce theological disputations to settle assorted doctrinal differences and establish robust doctrinal orthodoxy. This ferment unleashed a wave of theological movements and schools strong enough to influence subsequent centuries of Christian development.

Looking back several centuries, Christianity in North Africa, particularly in the Coptic tradition, gave the world church two things that have survived in the history of the church: the first, a new way of witnessing to the summons of the gospel in the form of monasticism and eremetism; and the second, a platform for debate, development, and the establishment of doctrinal orthodoxy through the practice of conversation. The former has survived creditably well; the latter has known a checkered history.

To date, it is impossible to separate the role of Christian North Africa from the emergence, development, and codification of the central articulations of Christian beliefs, the most notable of which are the christological and trinitarian dogmas and creedal statements. Although only a remnant of North African Christianity exists today, its theological, doctrinal, and dogmatic legacy remains indelible.

Slightly above the equator on the eastern tip of Africa, another equally fascinating Christian tradition was fashioned. According to the narrative, the main protagonist was the biblical Queen Saba who visited the scion and sage of the Davidic dynasty, King Solomon, in Israel, and returned pregnant. Through the inadvertent ingenuity of Solomon's offspring, Menelik, the founder of Ethiopia's imperial dynasty, the Ark of the Covenant eventually found its way to Ethiopia. This is the gist of the legend recorded in the famous chronicle *Kebra Negast* (Glory of the Kings) of the royal dynasties of Ethiopia. A variant suggests that the king made a gift of the ark to the queen. We will never know what really happened.

According to the biblical account, the ark was no ordinary object. It was the outcome of God's special command to Moses and was to be the revered repository of two stone tablets on which the Ten Commandments of God were etched. It sealed the covenant between God and the people of Israel who were newly liberated from slavery in Egypt. Where the ark was, there was God in all of God's awesome glory and blazing splendor. Steven Spielberg's 1981 blockbuster movie *Raiders of the Lost Ark* tells a spectacular and vivid story of the significance and potency of the biblical ark.

In the stone chapel of Aksum, nestled in the northern highlands of Ethiopia, a lone virgin monk stands guard over the ark, known to Ethiopian Christians as *Tabota Seyen*. He lives and dies in the presence of the ark. No one has ever seen the ark, and no one is supposed to see it except for the succession of lone virgin guardians. This object of ancient mystery is at the heart of one of the most spectacular religious feasts, called *Timkat*, celebrating the Epiphany in the Ethiopian Orthodox tradition.

The singular act of imperial romance between Saba and Solomon set off a chain of events in which Ethiopia's Judeo-Christian traditions are firmly anchored. The origins of the Ethiopian Orthodox Church are Coptic, but its roots are Judaic, blending Egyptian and Syriac influences. The early fourth century was the decisive moment. Historically, Saint Frumentius or Abba Salama (Father of Peace), the first bishop of Aksum, and Saint Edesius are credited with the evangelization of Ethiopia and the foundation of the Orthodox Church. But the narrative of the Ethiopian eunuch in Acts 8:26 is also claimed as a historical catalyst for the launch of Ethiopia's evangelization. For several centuries, theologically, liturgically, and doctrinally the umbilical cord of Christian Ethiopia was firmly attached to the Egyptian church. The historical severance of this umbilical cord happened in 1959 when the Ethiopian church began appointing its own supreme leader, *Abuna*, from among national clerics.

These two highly simplified legends of Mark and Saba demonstrate one fact. The story of Christianity in Africa is not pure history, but evolution. If history presupposes linearity of account, evolution reveals mutation of strains and the critical importance of adaptation for survival. Ironically, though, due to a series of historical events, neither of these two traditions evolved significantly. Under the overbearing pressure of an Islamic invasion and domination, the Egyptian Coptic Church survived in a theological, ecclesiological, and doctrinal bubble. With the passage of time this church experienced outright persecution and martyrdom orchestrated by extreme terrorism masked as religious ideology.

The doctrinal progeny of the Coptic Church, the Ethiopian Orthodox Tewahido Church (EOTC), also faced similar threats, in addition to relentless attempts by European missionaries, including the Jesuits, to penetrate its fortified religious frontiers. Ethiopia succeeded to a large extent in repelling foreign missionary advances, but with two unintended consequences. First, it became isolated from global Christianity and, second, it gloried in its religious exceptionality, but barely registered any significant impact beyond its national and traditional pool of membership. Meanwhile, the glories of the Ethiopian Orthodox Church continue to manifest themselves in its rich archaeological, psalmodic, poetic, hagiographical, and linguistic heritage. It should be noted, however, that, there are thriving migrant communities of EOTC in various parts of the world. Next door in Kenya, for example, members are easily recognized by their simple woven white shawls and tunics as they gather for or disperse from worship.

The near elimination of Christianity in North Africa and the exotic glorification of its Ethiopian branch did not generate any significant impetus to develop and grow Christianity in sub-Saharan Africa in subsequent centuries. Although strong within their respective national bases and boasting migrant communities in the diaspora, neither of the two historic traditions accounts for the astronomical growth of Christianity that Africa has witnessed in the twentieth and twenty-first centuries.

The Missionaries Are Coming

The near elimination of Christianity in North Africa and the exotic inertia of the Ethiopian church did not bode well for the development and growth of Christianity in Africa in subsequent centuries. That would change from the fifteenth through the seventeenth centuries when intrepid European state-sponsored seafarers, merchants, and fortune hunters, often dressed as accredited explorers and ambassadors, began to venture abroad in search of the mysteries and bounties of the Dark Continent. On the back of these daring expeditions rode Christian missionaries. Over the course of three centuries, European missionaries disembarked along coastal Africa under the patronage of colonial officials. Colonialism and Christianity operated like the proverbial two hands: each washing the other as mutually complementary and reinforcing enterprises.

The colonial and missionary expeditions of the fifteenth, sixteenth, and seventeenth centuries produced a distinctive strain of Christianity focused on traditional African rulers, namely, "Christian court civilization." Multiple historical examples include the Kongo kingdom of present-day Angola and the Democratic Republic of Congo (DRC), and strings of monarchies along the coast of West Africa, in places like the kingdoms of Abomey, Ashanti, Benin, and Warri. "Court Christianity" survived for at least two centuries, but it did not really take root. That is hardly surprising. As the label suggests, at best it was the preferred pastime of monarchical elites; at worst, it was a useful strategy of political expediency.

As a missionary strategy, court Christianity rested on a simple premise. Because the political arrangement in middle Africa from 1500 to 1800 vested near-absolute power in kings, chieftains, suzerains, and ruling elites, who also appropriated and exercised religious authority, missionaries assumed that the conversion of the rulers and elite would catalytically trigger the conversion of their entire population. In other words, the religion of the rulers would determine the religion of their subjects. Without a doubt, this strategy was a direct transplantation of the medieval political principle of *cuius regio, eius religio*. In hindsight, this stratagem proved to be a serious miscalculation and left a historical scar on the credibility of the Christian mission in Africa.

The ruling elites, especially the kings, were not naïve. By their own calculation, an alliance with missionaries and a nominal conversion significantly enhanced their eligibility for military support and their access to favorable commercial transactions with colonial powers. This much coveted arrangement ensured dominance, or the perception of it, over and against political rivals. Perhaps the greatest harm to the missionary enterprise, of which the agents of Christianity would certainly have been aware, was that the ruling elites also constituted economic blocs that bartered goods in return for exotic European luxuries and articles. For over three centuries, those goods, sadly, comprised mostly human cargo. Thus, by virtue of its predilection for court recognition, Christianity in Africa courted and incurred historical censure for complicity in the abhorrent and illegal trade in human beings.

To this day, vestiges of this failed strain of Christian civilization abound in several parts of Africa. Examples include the courtly vestments of palace chiefs and a national shrine of Aruosa in Benin City, and the Portuguese names and titles of kings in the annals of the defunct Kongo kingdom.

At the end of the eighteenth century at least three strains of Christian presence were present in Africa: Coptic North Africa, Ethiopian Tewahido, and court Christianity. The first was struggling for survival engulfed by a flourishing but hostile Islamic civilization; the second was confined within national boundaries as the religion of state in Ethiopia (a status it had since 333 CE); and the last had all but disappeared as the royal patrons were toppled by colonial powers who propped up their Christian regimes. A new strain of Christianity was in the making that would transform the fortunes of Christianity in Africa for good (or for worse).

Let the Scramble Begin

The nineteenth century witnessed the emergence of a new wave of evangelization in Africa, namely, missionary Christianity. Colonial expansion was gathering momentum and explorers were daring further afield into hinterlands beyond the coastal havens. Not to be outdone by these secular adventurers, European Christian establishments were also deter-

mined to go further inland. After all theirs was a divine commission to preach the "Good News" to the ends of the earth.
As in previous centuries, there was a strong and intentional
entanglement between Christian missionaries and the European colonial enterprise in Africa from the late eighteenth
century through the early twentieth century. The renowned
historian of African Christianity Elizabeth Isichei has observed
that in many parts of Africa, the local names for missionaries
were synonymous with the term "white man." For the Ganda,
Catholic missionaries were simply French or *baFranza*, and
their Protestant counterparts English or *baIngereeza*. In my
mother tongue the word *Efada* ([reverend] "father") was used
to translate "white man." Although "father" represented cross
and "white man" represented crown, they were one and the
same in the eyes of the people.

Missionary Christianity inaugurated a denominational
scramble for Africa. In Africa's history, the term "scramble"
is highly emotive and evocative. I use it deliberately to tie the
missionary enterprise to another contemporary and equally
defining episode in the history of Africa, namely, the partition of Africa by colonialist and imperialist Europe. The latter event, recorded in history as the Berlin Conference of
1884–85, had one objective: to accord legitimacy to European
territorial claims in Africa. It resulted in the partition of the
continent along commercial, economic, and political lines. In
reality, the colonial powers did a great service to Christian
missionaries. The denominational partition and scramble for
Africa paralleled the colonial political process. It represented
one of the striking feats of the European missionary societies. With the political map of Africa newly drawn, missionary
societies mapped out their overseas territories to renew their
evangelical foray into Africa.

Although the evangelical imagination of the Protestant
mission societies (Baptist, Anglican, Wesleyan, Methodist,
Lutheran, Reformed, Presbyterian, and so on) hardly exceeded

the horizon of the Great Commission (Matt 28:16-20), theirs was a monumental project that heralded the advent of a new society in Africa. Undeterred by the menace of tropical diseases, countless missionary stalwarts, enthusiasts, zealots, adventurers, and foot-soldiers fanned out across southern, eastern, western, and central Africa on an apostolic mission to establish a new Christian civilization cast solidly in the mold of European Christianity.

On the side of the Roman Catholic Church, the evangelizing project was conceived and steered by missionary congregations that proliferated in the nineteenth century, many if not all of which have survived to date. The list would include the Society of African Missions, the Holy Ghost Fathers (aka the Spiritans), the Missionaries of Africa (aka the White Fathers), the Oblates of Mary Immaculate, the Verona Fathers and Sisters (aka the Comboni), the Sisters of Notre Dame de Namur, the Sisters of St. Joseph of Cluny, and many more.

One aspect of this evangelizing enterprise in sub-Saharan Africa is striking. Notwithstanding a certain tension, by and large Africa proved stupendously receptive to the proposition of missionary Christianity. But "reception" might be too tame a word. Not only did African communities receive Christianity as proposed by missionaries, even in instances where it was imposed by force of arms or guile of gifts, they also interpreted and translated it according to their indigenous religious beliefs, imagination, and consciousness, that which I identify generically as African Religion. This factor accounts in part for the origin and unique features of the African independent/instituted churches.

The effort and success of Protestant and Catholic missionaries in establishing denominational churches would eventually spawn such independent, African-led Christian communities in the late nineteenth and early twentieth centuries. A few names come to mind: *Ibandla lamaNazaretha* or the Nazareth Baptist Church in South Africa founded by Isaiah Mloyiswa

Mdliwamafa Shembe (1870–1935); the Zion Christian Church also in South Africa founded by Engenas Barnabas Lekganyane (1885–1948); and the Celestial Church of Christ in Nigeria founded by Samuel Bilehou Joseph Oshoffa (1909–1985).

These homebred communities were the precursors of modern-day African megachurches. In their heyday they spanned vast geographical territories. Accordingly, they were the object of special interest by the colonial powers for the influence they wielded over the masses of common folks. In their struggle for an emancipated and autonomous Christian church, these communities adopted codes of conduct and standards of practice that tended to prioritize the Old Testament over the New Testament, based in part on their claim of a certain affinity between biblical Judaic practices such as polygamy and ritual animal sacrifices and indigenous African religious traditions and values.

This abridged narrative identifies several evolutionary strains of Christianity in Africa: Coptic-orthodox, Ethiopian-orthodox, Portuguese-court, European-missionary societies and congregations, and African-independent. Then in the early twentieth-century North American Pentecostalism led to the emergence of Pentecostal and charismatic strains of Christianity in Africa. A great deal of literature and solid scholarship exists on these latter-day strains of Christianity in Africa. I will focus more explicitly on them in the chapter 4.

Reading between the Lines

The assortment and combination of strains of missionary histories have resulted in a stupendous reality in the twenty-first century: the astronomical growth of Christianity in Africa. This development is the subject of many glowing reviews of the progress, prospects, and promises of Christianity in Africa for the world church. I have already noted the important surveys conducted by the Pew Forum on Religion and Public Life and Georgetown University's Center for Applied Research in the Apostolate. As do several other surveys and studies, both reports conclude on a positive note—Christianity in Africa is of vital importance for the future survival of the global Christian community. The future of global Christianity will pass through Africa.

The responses to this phenomenon of growth range from amazement to wonder, celebration to jubilation. Cardinal Theodore McCarrick, archbishop emeritus of Washington, D.C., and chair of the United States Conference of Catholic Bishops' Subcommittee on the Church in Africa, once declared: "The growth of the church in Africa is a gift to the Church as a whole."

Although I have used the word "miracle" in the title of this chapter, this is a somewhat misleading characterization of a century of dramatic expansion of Christianity in Africa. As I understand and use it, "miracle" is not intended to adduce divine intervention or credit supernatural agency for the flourishing of the Christian enterprise in twenty-first-century Africa. Human instrumentation and ingenuity are more likely key factors in the evolution, survival, and expansion of Christianity in Africa during the last century and in the present.

Judging from their perceptions, prejudices, and stereotypes, the missionaries did not expect much fruit from their arduous and death-defying evangelical labors. For the average missionary setting off for Africa in the nineteenth century, the typecasting of Africa as "the White man's grave" was a widely diffused and deeply engrained phenomenon. Such nomenclature was not mere metaphor. The combination of rampant malaria and other tropical diseases ensured frighteningly elevated mortality rates among colonial and missionary Europeans, even as they introduced diseases previously unknown among African populations. Kwasi Kwarteng's acerbic account of the socioeconomic and political hubris and horrors of the British Empire across the globe, and its aftereffect, mentions how "Nigerians would joke that the mosquito should be recognized as a national hero, as it has prevented the mass arrival of white

settlers, which, no doubt, smoothed Nigeria's political path."[3]
Early missionary bulletins, memoirs, and field correspondence
report in vivid images their encounters with cannibals, heathens, and savages, dark of body, mind, and soul.

Understandably, for many, under those circumstances, proselytization was akin to mounting daring raids into the cursed
stronghold of the Devil. Even stalwarts, like Charles Lavigerie
(1825–1892), founder of the White Fathers, came to believe
that converting a people with no religion, no ideas of God, and
no morality was a losing battle, for which he was willing to
accept but the slimmest tokens of conversion as recompense.

Beware of Gifts

Three related issues should be considered in any discussion
of the conversion of Africa. The first is an etiological question:
What accounts for the phenomenal conversion of Africans to
Christianity, and the astronomical rise in the number of Christians on the continent in the last hundred years? I believe that
the answer is not as sophisticated as historians of religion,
sociologists, and anthropologists make it out to be.[4] Second,
I undertake a critique of the fascination with the statistical
growth of Christianity in Africa. My concern is to show that—
in both theological accounts and scientific surveys—we need
a more realistic and critical assessment of the phenomenon of
growth before it can be advanced as the basis for considering
it a gift to the world church. Third, I propose a hypothesis on
why the world church can continue to count on the growth of
Christianity in Africa for the foreseeable future.

The Mode of the Receiver

At least three considerations are worth noting about the
astronomical rise in the number of Christians on the continent
in the last hundred years. First, aside from heroic attempts
by missionaries to endear the faith to royal courts under the

patronage of imperialist Europe, the first real converts to Christianity, especially during the third missionary wave in the nineteenth and twentieth centuries, were socially marginalized, economically impoverished, and culturally disempowered women, men, and children. Such was the lot of the majority of the Africans who flocked to savior-personalities like Isaiah Shembe and Samuel Oshoffa. In reality, Christianity in modern Africa did not take root and spread from the centers of political power, as the early missionaries had planned and hoped for. Rather it evolved in the craters of Christian villages, mission outposts, and mission houses, the vast majority of which were refuges and safe havens for social rejects or, in the apt depiction of the eminent historian of Christianity in Africa, Adrian Hastings, "the dregs of African society."[5] They included the physically disabled, lepers, mothers of twins, the widowed, the childless, and ex-slaves—in short "those to whom the traditional world offered little happiness."[6]

Interestingly, these so-called dregs and marginal Christians were the first Africans to reap en masse the benefits of missionary Christianity in the forms of education, healthcare, and catechetical instruction. Historians of Christianity in Africa routinely criticize this missionary strategy for opting to create an alternative society instead of prophetically denouncing unjust and oppressive social structures. There is merit to this criticism. Yet we cannot deny the fact that, in effect, albeit unwittingly, Christianity was changing society from the fringes and margins of the continent. Whereas the ruling class and elites cast a disdainful eye upon this religion of the poor, ex-slaves, and outcasts, these latter would become the first beneficiaries of Western literacy, numeracy, and other vital skills coveted in the running of the colonial administrative machinery and the aftermath of nationalism and independence.

In point of fact, Christianity in Africa has preserved this historical memory, because it continues to appeal to the poor, with the notable difference that poverty is no longer considered the blissful state of blessedness extolled in the gospel beatitudes, but a reversible condition by which the sowing of faith can achieve socioeconomic prosperity. I shall return to this point shortly.

A second consideration is that the success and prosperity of Christianity in Africa are rooted in the religion's adaptive instincts. The strongest surviving strains are those that did not exhaust themselves in the futile preservation of antiquated legends, but that exploited the opportunity to extend their communities among the vast African populations. In business-speak the Christian leaders saw a huge market potential and took their chance. Protestant and Catholic missionaries suffered no crisis of conscience in understanding their mission as proselytization, even if it meant drawing on the support of the colonial state. Present-day Pentecostals, evangelicals, charismatics, and African independent churches can hardly be qualified as bashful or diffident when it comes to the active pursuit and recruitment of new members. The pursuit of new members is an intensely competitive evangelical task. The methods of recruitment demonstrate sophistication, ingenuity, and innovation, especially when propelled by the digital revolution and the sustained rise of social media. The extent to which certain evangelical methods strengthen or distort the Christian message is a topic for a later chapter.

That the surviving strains of missionary Christianity shared some fundamental commonalities is a third consideration. They prioritized scripture as an eminently translatable and widely accessible narrative that would accord converts the facility and capability not simply to recite and parrot it, but to retell and appropriate the Christian story in their local and familiar tongues and to adapt it to their context. Evidently this process entails selectivity and creativity on the part of the converted Africans. In its attenuated form, this notion of translatability, propounded and popularized by Gambian scholar Lamin Sanneh, has metamorphosed from adaptation or contextualization to inculturation. Tanzanian theologian Laurenti Magesa has demonstrated in his study that inculturation is a mutually enriching and critical process whereby the gospel takes on the voice, tone, and texture of the local context or community and the community in turn reinterprets the message of the gospel in fresh new ways.[7] The pioneers of the African independent churches would have agreed with this definition.

These three considerations are either noticeably missing or recessive in the evolution of Coptic and Ethiopian Christian traditions. For this reason, I disagree with the claim by renowned church historian Adrian Hastings that "in undeniable fashion, fourth-century Egyptian Christianity was to be paradigmatic for the Africa of the future."[8] I view this as a historical exaggeration. Considered historically, theologically, and liturgically, the terms and thesis of such a monumental claim remain unproven.

Numbers Don't Lie?

I have a second concern with statistics. As suggested above, many scholars know, judge, and relate to Christian Africa in purely statistical terms. There is no doubt that the numbers are compelling. However, from the critical perspective of being a convert myself, this preoccupation borders on an obsession and a triumphalism that impedes a critical evaluation and understanding of the importance of Christianity in Africa for the global Christian community.

In previous published research and scholarship, I have quoted statistics to demonstrate the "miraculous" growth of Christianity. However, recent patterns of growth and evolution convince me that numbers alone do not tell the complete story of Christianity in Africa. In fact, numbers make for anemic accounts rather than full-blooded narratives of the progress, prospects, and promises of Christianity in Africa. Hence I feel a need to qualify and critique this obsession with statistics that has been the cornerstone of numerous scholarly appraisals of Christianity in Africa.

Besides, as statisticians and social scientists know too well, collecting data on Christian communities in Africa is a notoriously frustrating exercise. These communities are in a perpetual process of self-replication and mutation. At best, statistics on Christian religious movements in Africa allow us to make educated guesses.

The key question remains: How can we measure and assess the expansion of Christianity in Africa? Following the line of my argument, if statistics and demographics are precise tools of measurement that objectively interpret the reality of Christianity in Africa in terms of growth or decline, expansion cannot simply be reduced to a material and impersonal process. At its core Christianity is not a matter of counting bodies, masses, and throngs of worshipers entering and exiting sites of religious worship; it must have reference to their *lived experience*.

Already in the 1960s, Adrian Hastings considered the rapid expansion of Christianity a problem for the church and predicted that "the mass conversion which has been characteristic of much of mission work in the still recent past will have less and less place in the future."[9] That was more than fifty years ago, and the eminent church historian's prediction did not quite materialize, or at least not as he may have intended it. The current growth of Christianity is massive, and the number of conversions (counted by the number of baptisms) is significant. Perhaps the true import of Hastings's observation lies in a salutary caution against relying too heavily and uncritically on statistics and demography to gauge the salience, relevance, and vitality of Christianity in Africa today. I believe that such caution still retains its validity.

Statistics can be reductionist. In reality, statistics can be used to demonstrate a simple juxtaposition of the decline in church attendance and religious self-identification in the northern hemisphere with the packed and overflowing church pews in the southern hemisphere. To portray this in vivid terms, it is as if—on a balance—the numerical preponderance of Christianity in the global South is tilting the scales southward, leaving the global North dangling dangerously.

If we take a long view of history and, particularly, adopt an evolutionary perspective, this present reality of Christianity in Africa is part of a long process of the development of global Christianity, not a one-off demographic or statistical fluke.

From statistics, scholars routinely draw conclusions about the vitality of Christianity in Africa. And here lies another myth, the myth of vitality. The nineteen-country survey of Islam and Christianity in sub-Saharan Africa by the Pew Forum on Religion and Public Life cited above concludes:

> Indeed, sub-Saharan Africa is clearly among the most religious places in the world. In many countries across the continent, roughly nine-in-ten people or more say religion is *very important* in their lives. By this key measure, even the least religiously inclined nations in the region score higher than the United States, which is among the most religious of the advanced industrial countries.[10]

Likewise, the CARA report notes in its introductory lines: "Arguably, the three most important indicators of 'vitality' for the Catholic Church are the number of Catholics, the number of parishes, and the number of priests."

To measure religious vitality, social science surveys typically tabulate church attendance figures and collate self-reports of respondents regarding their personal affiliation, observance, and devotion. Besides the subjectivity of evaluations inherent in this method, the inquirer usually overreaches the boundaries of investigation to reach conclusions on matters such as the vitality and vibrancy of religious life.

By focusing on these external indicators we miss important questions that arise on account of the nature of Christianity itself. Although Christianity shows measurable trends, it does not make a fashion statement; it makes a claim that transformation is possible for believers and their social structures. Emmanuel Katongole argues in his important work *The Sacrifice of Africa* that in addition to church attendance and devotion, it is important to probe the extent to which, for example, Christianity in Africa lives up to this claim by promoting human flourishing, social transformation, economic development, and a transformative political imagination.[11] Statistical studies and surveys do not answer these questions, which I am convinced offer more compelling criteria for assessing the importance of Christianity in Africa for the world church.

Statistical studies yield one final myth, namely, the myth of homogeneity. In Africa, Christianity is growing in different directions and this growth pattern is seldom uniform. There are important variations among countries and within countries that we may miss in our fixation on numbers. Consider, for example, the basic variable of weekly attendance at Catholic Masses. In Nigeria attendance in 2011 reached 92 percent. Compare that to South Africa at 38 percent in the same year. Similar variations have been observed within and among countries in Africa.[12]

In the final analysis, my critique hinges on one single word, growth. Is growth simply a function of numbers? For some theologians, statisticians, sociologists, and historians, numbers are the single most important indicator of progress. I hold the position that scholars, especially those who approach the question from the perspective of theology and ethics, ought to be more alert to the limitations and pitfalls of numbers.

If we return for a moment to the ruins of North African Christianity, the contributions of Africa to world Christianity were hardly based on its statistical or demographic preponderance. What counted most was the quality of scholarship, the depth of Christian commitment (there were more African saints and martyrs in the first five hundred years than in the last fifteen hundred years!), and a pioneering spirit that engendered new forms of Christian living and movements like monasticism. The "genes" of this extinct tradition have mutated dramatically, but they still have traits that survive and thrive in strains of present-day Christianity in Africa. Granted, circumstances and contexts are markedly different, but if we apply the criteria of the depth and durability of its theological impact, Christian commitment, and innovative witnessing, I must conclude that some contemporary strains appear recessive rather than progressive. And—as should be evident by now—my purpose is not to hanker after any glorious legends of Africa's Christian past.

Many conclusions can be drawn from this condensed narrative of the promises and myths of Christianity in Africa. First, quite clearly, Christianity in Africa has never been a monolithic phenomenon. At the dawn of missionary Christianity, observes Elizabeth Isichei, "There were many Christianities, as there were many African host societies."[13] What was true then remains even more so today. Current taxonomy lags behind the rapid mutation of Christian communities in Africa.

Second, the narrative of Christianity does not follow a straight and linear trajectory. There are legends and myths, twist and turns, episodes and events, surprises and promises, discoveries and dead ends in enough stupefying abundance to justify Pliny the Elder's famous declaration *ex Africa semper aliquid novi!*

Finally, Christianity in Africa was not an accident of history, but an evolution of converging world events, processes, and intriguing personalities across a multiplicity of geographical locations.

What we see today as a flourishing religion is a blossoming of seeds sown at the dawn of the Christian century, the most resilient and dominant strains of which were exported from Europe, beginning in the eighteenth century, and planted in the soil of African religious traditions. Anything before that turned out to be too fragile or too vulnerable to internal weaknesses and external threats from rivals and competitors, with Islam being the most formidable. The importance of this religion for the religious consciousness of many Africans will form part of the focus of the next chapter.

Notes

1. Center for Applied Research in the Apostolate (CARA) at George-town University, *Global Catholicism: Trends & Forecasts* (June 4, 2015).

2. Elizabeth Isichei, *A History of Christianity in Africa: From Antiquity to the Present* (Grand Rapids, MI: Eerdmanns, 1995), 17.

3. Kwasi Kwarteng, *Ghosts of Empire: Britain's Legacies in the Modern World* (London: Bloomsbury, 2011), 286.

4. I think here, for example, of Robin Horton's spirited attempts in the 1970s to explain "African conversion" by adducing a theory of natural progression from a restricted microcosmic context or enclave to exposure to a wider macrocosmic context of world religions, like Islam and Christianity. See Robin Horton, "African Traditional Thought and Western Science," *Africa* 37 (1967): 50–71; "African Conversion," *Africa* 41 (1971): 85–108; "On the Rationality of Conversion (Part 1)," *Africa* 45 (1975): 219–35; "On the Rationality of Conversion (Part 2)," *Africa* 45 (1975): 373–99; Robin Horton and J. D. Y. Peel, "Conversion and Confusion: A Rejoinder on Christianity in Eastern Nigeria," *Canadian Journal of African Studies* 10, no. 3 (1976): 481–98.

5. Adrian Hastings, *Church & Mission in Modern Africa* (London: Burns & Oates, 1967).

6. Isichei, *A History of Christianity in Africa*, 134; see 156–57; 168–70.

7. Laurenti Magesa, *Anatomy of Inculturation: Transforming the Church in Africa* (Maryknoll, NY: Orbis Books, 2004), 9–76.

8. Adrian Hastings, *The Church in Africa, 1450–1950* (Oxford: Oxford University Press, 1996), 6.

9. Hastings, *Church & Mission in Modern Africa*, 49.

10. Pew Forum, "Tolerance and Tension: Islam and Christianity in Sub-Saharan Africa," 2010 (http://www.pewforum.org/files/2010/04/sub-saharan-africa-full-report.pdf).

11. Emmanuel Katongole, *The Sacrifice of Africa: A Political Theology of Africa* (Grand Rapids, MI: Eerdmanns, 2011), 7–20; 41–50; 51ff.

12. Center for Applied Research in the Apostolate, *Global Catholicism*, 26.

13. Isichei, *A History of Christianity in Africa*, 88.

3

A Marketplace of Faiths

The world is divided into people who have wit
and no religion and people who have religion
and no wit.

—*Avicenna*

The following account by Ugandan theologian Emmanuel
Katongole, currently a professor at the University of Notre
Dame, on a visit to West Africa provides the backdrop for this
chapter's focus on religious claims, contestations, and conflicts
in Africa.

I found myself unable to sleep as my room felt like
a sound box: the church had a night vigil going; the
nearby market hosted a disco; on the other side of the
Catholic Church, the Assemblies of God had an all-
night prayer session. At four o'clock in the morning, the
Muslim muezzin joined in with a call to prayer. What
particularly irritated and deeply annoyed me was the
fact that each of these "congregations" was not content
with simply addressing their congregations: their speak-
ers were mounted outside on their sanctuaries, and it
was as if each congregation was trying to outshout the

> other. In fact, what the . . . experience confirmed was
> the reality of post-colonial Africa as a market place of
> competing [religious] ideologies, each trying to drown
> out the other.[1]

For people who know Africa, the professor's experience
is as pervasive as it is unexceptional in the continent's burgeoning marketplace of religious ideologies. As we have seen,
observers, researchers, and analysts celebrate the religious
effervescence of the continent. Also, as I pointed out in the
previous chapter, and will do so repeatedly, an uncritical focus
on the numerical dimensions of this growth risks occluding the
less than complimentary aspects of religious performance. My
principal aim in this chapter is to probe some of the dynamics
of religious traditions in Africa. I focus on claims, contestations, and conflicts, leaving aside, at least for now, the more
heartening subjects of cooperation, collaboration, and coexistence, examples of which are also numerous.

To recall a piece of recent history briefly mentioned in the
first chapter, on October 4, 2009, in St. Peter's Basilica at the
Vatican, Emeritus Pope Benedict XVI, presiding at the Eucha-
rist for the inauguration of the Second Special Assembly for
Africa of the Synod of Bishops, summed up in glowing tribute
the religious legacy of Africa for the world. "Africa," Benedict declared, "represents an enormous spiritual 'lung' for a
humanity that appears to be in a crisis of faith and hope." He
promptly appended a caveat, saying, "But this 'lung' can take
ill as well."

The pope identified "at least two dangerous pathologies"
that threaten the spiritual wellbeing of Africa. First, the West
with its "form of sickness of the spirit" appears to be export-
ing its "spiritual toxic" waste of "practical materialism combined with relativist and nihilist thinking," and contaminating
the peoples of other continents, particularly in Africa. Benedict identified a second threat, labelling it a "'virus' that could
hit Africa, that is, religious fundamentalism, mixed together

with political and economic interests." He described the menace posed by this virus in the following terms: "Groups who follow various religious creeds are spreading throughout the continent of Africa: they do so in God's name, but following a logic that is opposed to divine logic, that is, teaching and practicing not love and respect for freedom, but intolerance and violence."[2]

Names bring about division. Benedict was careful not to disclose names, although there could be little doubt about the identity of the peddlers of the logic of violence in the name of faith. As elsewhere, Africa is home to a plethora of groups or movements that claim religious inspiration for assorted forms of terror, banditry, exploitation, and criminality. The virus has already hit the continent.

Much can be said about the historical origins, distinct paths, evolution, and transformation of Africa's triple religious heritage. The preceding chapter explored the origins and evolution of Christianity in Africa. As part of the present narrative of religious claims, contestations, and conflicts present on the continent, I would now like to offer a sketch of the historical development of Islam in Africa. This brief treatment of Islam is not exhaustive, but it should prepare the stage for my argument that Christianity and Islam flourish on a ground saturated with the values and principles of African Religion. In other words, the stone that was routinely rejected and roundly condemned as animist may have a more significant influence on these religions than is officially admitted.

What's in a Name?

I have made my peace with the term "African Religion," even though I am convinced that it falls short of capturing the deeper sense and meaning of the African religious imagination in which I was schooled and that I identify as our way of life. Although African Religion is variously qualified as indigenous, autochthonous, primal, or traditional, historians, theologians, and anthropologists are divided on whether to consider this phenomenon a singular or plural reality. Besides, without qualification, the commonly preferred adjective "traditional" carries the obvious connotation of passé, antiquated, and outmoded. African Religion is anything but.

Laurenti Magesa, who wields considerable authority on this matter, argues—and to my mind, convincingly—that there is only one African Religion that is manifested in a variety of forms across diverse cultural and geographical locations on the continent and beyond.[3] Without rehashing his argument, I use the term African Religion consistently in this book. It helps the narrative and provides a common language for the purposes of conversation.

Magesa further argues—though, I think, less convincingly—in favor of considering African Religion a world religion.[4] However, the fact that thriving expressions of this religion are firmly established in African diasporan communities lends credence to Magesa's claim. Some of the notable religious traditions that trace their origins to sub-Saharan Africa include Candomblé in Brazil, Santería in Cuba, and Vodun in Haïti.

A second pertinent consideration concerns the nature of African Religion itself and the manner in which it has been studied. As available literature indicates, African Religion is hardly if ever studied from the inside, that is, by its self-declared practitioners and adherents. By this same token, the reader might question my credentials for conducting this present analysis. The narrative in chapter 1 should have answered this query satisfactorily. As I have pointed out, no matter how many times a leopard crosses a river, it never loses its spots.

As noted in chapter 1, African Religion does not identify itself as "religion," that is, having an organized system of worship and belief based on a set of defining characteristics that fit into a neatly defined category of analysis. Yet it is important to point out that such an absence, at least in the early scholarly discourse and study of religion in Africa, can be attributed at least in part to the missionary strategy of denying rationality, morality, and religious consciousness to Africans, thus justifying the missionaries' attempt to extirpate their forms of belief and impose Christianity. In my opinion, the problem is not simply a matter of nomenclature but of the nature of the object and the appropriate tools of research.

Nonetheless, some exponents and historians of religion in Africa have identified a handful of characteristics by which African Religion is defined. These features complement the description presented in the introductory chapter and include the following:

- a two-tier structure of belief that recognizes the supremacy of an Ultimate Reality or Being, assisted by a coterie of so-called lesser, smaller, auxiliary, economic gods and goddesses, or agents;
- a cosmological worldview that structures levels of existence on a grid of the visible material realm and the invisible spiritual realm, where spiritual beings and human beings interact either to advance or to hinder the wellbeing of the living;
- a space where through a series of ritual practices human beings attempt to harness, channel, or neutralize the implicit powers of spiritual beings as a means of coping with diverse situations and conditions in life, from birth through death;
- an ethical framework that prioritizes life and judges human action in the measure that it strengthens or weakens the force of life;
- an intense preoccupation with health, wellbeing, and wholeness that accords devotees a multiplicity of means to fortify and protect themselves from external threats;
- the use of symbols and art to embody, portray, and transmit values and beliefs.

Apart from these characteristics, among the most salient features of this religious tradition are that, unlike Christianity and Islam, it is not a text-based religion. Its beliefs and practices, rituals and rites are a matter of cultic practices embodied in symbolic re-enactments and are subject to ongoing interpretation, reconstruction, and transformation. African Religion does not speak through the medium of canonized scripture, official doctrine, or codified creed, much less solemnized dogma. In somewhat analogous terms, its "texts" are those ritualized and sacralized gestures in cultic spaces and in everyday living. However, despite the fact that African Religion is not based on a historical revelation, like Christianity and Islam, it is not a-historical. The symbolic re-enactment of culturally relevant rituals and the reconstruction of their meaning follows a cyclical rhythm based on concrete experiences, such as birth, work, community, diminishment, death, and return.

Secondly, unlike Christianity and Islam, African Religion eschews proselytization. This feature is of paramount importance, considering that the explicit aim of Christianity and Islam was to discredit, diminish, and dislodge African Religion through an aggressive evangelical program of conversion.

What about Islam?

Islam appeared in Africa from the Arabian Peninsula seven years after the death of Prophet Muhammad in 632 CE. Weakened by internal doctrinal strife and political intrigue, the Egyptian Coptic Orthodox Church proved no match for the invading Arab forces. Although history records this event as a "military invasion," in a place like Egypt the encounter between a nascent Islam and a well-established Christian tradition was mitigated, among other factors, by Islam's adherence to the Qur'anic guarantee of protection for the so-called "Peoples of the Book," and also by a constructive interaction between Christian and Islamic theological scholars.

The first order of business for the invaders seemed not to be religious conversion but the establishment of a viable political regime. This political objective relied on the clerical expertise of local Christians and thus accommodated their linguistic and religious traditions. Over time, however, this initial benign arrangement of religious toleration and coexistence degenerated into hostility and persecution, to the point of reducing the Copts from their dominant position as a significant majority to a besieged minority.

The further westward expansion of Islam across Libya, Tunisia, and Algeria gradually consolidated its dominance as well as accelerated the diminishment of the presence and influence of Christianity in North Africa. Subsequent heroic attempts by Christian missionaries, like Charles Lavigerie, the founder of the White Fathers, to reverse the process never yielded the intended result. Meanwhile significant historical developments within and outside of Islam engendered a sophisticated tradition of scientific and humanistic scholarship (embodied in the works of renowned scholars like Al-Kindi [801–873], Avicenna [980–1037], and Averroes [1126–1198]), the proliferation of revivalist and reform movements, and the extension of Islam southward along the great trading routes into the Sahel region.

Besides trade and commerce, the trajectory of Islam's historical expansion followed clearly discernible political routes, including, notably, the phenomenon of *jihad*. The eighteenth- and nineteenth-century jihadist movements in the western part of Africa combined an explicit program of territorial conquest, economic expansion, and political dominance, and they were driven by an intense religious fervor. Islam as a religion was the driving force for the overthrow of existing political hegemonies and the establishment of vast theocratic states, comprising a string of powerful caliphates and emirates along the Sahel belt.

At the helm of these jihads were political and military leaders who doubled as religious leaders; one of the most prominent was Shehu Usman Dan Fodio (1754–1817), also known as the "Leader of the Faithful." It is interesting to note that, whether in Africa or elsewhere, the political persona, vocation, and strategy of several Muslim leaders struck a historical and ideological resonance with that of Muhammad, who, according to the insightful assessment of W. Montgomery Watt, was both a prophet and a statesman.[5]

Compared to Christianity, Islam presented no complicated set of doctrines or codes of belief to Africans. The process of conversion was equally simple, bolstered by the appeal of immediate integration into a universal religious and political community, the *umma* or brotherhood of shared interest and mutual protection that was defined not by consanguinity or ethnicity, but by common faith.

It is important to note some aspects of the historical evolution of Islam that are pertinent to the issue under consideration, even though what I offer here is not a comprehensive account. First, the exegesis of the term *jihad* in the Qur'an is a matter of debate and contention, and its spectrum ranges from a moderate striving to extreme violence. Unfortunately, it is the latter connotation that has stuck in the mind and imagination of many people. Second, even today many ancient conflicts and disagreements within Islam are still present; they concern the legitimacy of political succession, the preservation of tradition, and the orthodoxy of doctrine, notably between Shi'a and Sunni Muslims. Such divisions are a key factor in the intrareligious and interreligious conflicts in Africa and in other parts of the world. Third, influential state actors with hegemonic ambitions contribute to the tensions within Islam and between Muslims and people of other faiths in Africa, to the point that they resemble proxy wars. Fourth, within Islam, transnational organizations serve as focal points of unity and intrareligious and interreligious cooperation, such as the World Muslim Congress, the League of Arab States, and the Organization of Islamic Cooperation.

One outcome of the checkered evolution of religious traditions in Africa is a deep and "volatile religious fault line" that separates the predominantly Muslim North Africa from the predominantly Christian sub-Saharan Africa. Between the two halves lies—as described in the Pew report—"The great meeting place . . . a 4,000-mile swath from Somalia in the east to Senegal in the west."[6] Movements and shifts along this religious fault line separating the North from sub-Saharan Africa frequently erupt into violent sectarian conflagrations with devastating consequences. Despite this tension, judging by the Pew report, both Christianity and Islam have recorded favorable statistical and demographic patterns of growth:

> Since then [1900], however, the number of Muslims living between the Sahara Desert and the Cape of Good Hope has increased more than 20-fold, rising from an estimated 11 million in 1900 to approximately 234 million in 2010. . . . Sub-Saharan Africa now is home to about one-in-five of all the Christians in the world (21%) and more than one-in-seven of the world's Muslims (15%).[7]

This statistical data provides the rationale for a basic taxonomy of religious traditions in Africa that identifies three main groups: African Religion, Christianity, and Islam. Critically considered, this inventory rests on a premise that I consider problematic at best, or misleading at worst. When we pay close attention to the nature of these religions, the first thing that strikes the eye is the asymmetrical relationship among them. Christianity and Islam count their adherents in multiples of millions, and analysts of such statistics glibly conclude that African Religion is losing ground to these "world" religions. Here again the fallacy of relying on numbers obstructs any accurate analysis and obscures a clear perception of the reality of religious experience.

While there is no doubt about the numerical growth of Christianity and Islam, we must avoid the fallacy of concluding that African Religion is losing ground. As I have argued already, as I experienced African Religion from the perspective of a practitioner, the matter and practice of religion is inseparable from one's *way of life* in the same way that a leopard's spots cannot be erased by repeated dips in the river.

In reality, African Religion is the *ground* or sub-structure of the religious consciousness of Africans on which the other two religions have been superimposed over the course of time with varying degrees of compatibility. The relationship among them is not dictated by any numerical preponderance but by historical factors as well as the wider global context. The numbers of believers in Islam and Christianity may be blossoming, but the flowers are growing in a field sown with the beliefs and practices of African Religion.

Historian of religion Elizabeth Isichei, an expert in this field, has declared that "virtually all converts to Christianity [and Islam] in Africa have come from 'traditional' religions."[8] Her use of the term "come" presupposes an intentional transference of adherence and affiliation from one clearly defined religious tradition or space to another. Unfortunately Isichei juxtaposes African Religion, Christianity, and Islam and thus treats them as parallels. I find this problematic, although that this is a methodological staple in the study of religions in Africa. I will return to this question later.

Sowers and Reapers of Wrath

In various ways, at different times, and in several places, Christianity and Islam have manifested varying degrees of association with and a penchant for strategies infused with violence in their pursuit of specific goals. As I suggested earlier, in some parts of Africa, the advent of Christianity was almost always associated with the establishment of political systems by Western powers, which was disruptive, to say the least.

In the novel *Things Fall Apart*, one of Africa's best-known literary accounts of the encounter between African Religion and Western Christianity, Chinua Achebe puts the following words in the mouth of one of his characters, Obierika:

> But I am greatly afraid. We have heard stories about white men who made the powerful guns and the strong drinks and took slaves away across the seas, but no one thought the stories were true. . . .[9]

> But stories were already gaining ground that the white man had *not only brought a religion but also a government*. It was said that they had built a place of judgment in Umuofia to protect the followers of their religion. It was even said that they had hanged one man who killed a missionary.[10]

This somber account speaks volumes about the history of Christianity as a vehicle for the oftentimes repressive intrusion into the socioeconomic, political, cultural, and religious space of Africa. The association of Christianity with varying degrees of violence is, however, not a matter merely of a historical past. The legacies of this association persist in the pathological performance of some modern-day preachers of Christianity who, it must be said, cannot claim to be authentic exponents of the principles and practices of the religion.

In eastern Africa, for example, memory is still fresh of Alice Lakwena's chiliastic Holy Spirit Movement and its deranged progeny, Joseph Kony's Lord's Resistance Army in northern Uganda. Claiming biblical inspiration and divine revelation, both groups successfully mobilized their gullible membership to wreak havoc on innocent individuals and communities. The LRA killed, mutilated, abducted, and raped thousands of women, men, and children in northern Uganda. The gang was particularly notorious for its abhorrent practice of recruiting children into their ranks of bandits and abducting girls for use as sex slaves.

Fortunately, although Kony has not yet been captured, things are different today. On the very spot where the LRA leader Joseph Kony and his criminal gang used to barbeque cows that they stole from local communities, and on the bush path from which the LRA used to mount their deadly attacks, a school has been built by the Jesuits. Fittingly, this coeducational school is called *Ocer*—the local Acholi word for "Christ is risen." Where once death and violence decimated the lives of Ugandans, a new dawn is rising as children learn to build a better future. Rising from the ashes and debris of violence laced with religious ideology, the children of *Ocer* and other schools in northern Uganda no longer train for war; they are training for a better, bigger, and brighter future full of hope and promise. This story demonstrates the double-sided nature of religion as both pathological performance and transformative practice. These notions of practice and performance will be further elaborated in the next chapter.

The story of religious violence implicating Christianity continues to unfold. More recently, in Central African Republic, a militia movement, anti-balaka, has claimed Christian inspiration for its mortal combat with the Muslim movement of the Séléka. It is not surprising, then, that when Pope Benedict lambasts groups that follow the logic of violence under the pretext of promoting and advancing a divine cause, the finger not only points outward, but also inward. These groups are present in Christianity as well as in Islam.

In the case of Islam, contemporary movements that claim the religion as inspiration for their campaign of terror and violence include the schoolgirl-abducting jihadist group Boko Haram in Nigeria and neighboring countries; al-Shabaab in Somalia; and affiliates of al-Qaeda and the Islamic State of Iraq and the Levant dispersed across the Sahel and parts of North Africa. These are hardly isolated groups. As recent events demonstrate, they constitute a deadly transnational league of terrorist compacts, driven by the ruthless and depraved objective of creating a trans-border caliphate or state, leaving a wake of massive human rights abuses and crimes against humanity and cultural heritage.

Present-day extremist groups and militias, such as we find in Somalia, Chad, Libya, Tunisia, Egypt, Mali, Niger, Kenya, and Nigeria, for example, present competing claims for legitimacy. They are the political progenitors of degenerate historical movements that sought to create totalitarian political regimes across Africa, using violence to subjugate rivals, suppress resistance, and impose a harsh penal code on local populations. In some cases when religiously sanctioned laws have been imposed, public floggings, death by stoning, and the severance of limbs are considered acceptable punishment for infractions.

Whether in Christianity or Islam these groups apply various means to propagate extremist ideologies and inflict horrific violence on innocent individuals and communities. As some of the examples show, the spectrum of motivation ranges from revenge to banditry, a quest for power to the sadistic glorification of violence, and from economic interest to territorial conquest. Yet it would be simplistic to take the religious claims of these groups at face value. While their pursuit of violence may be dressed elaborately with the trappings and rhetoric of religion, the phenomenon is more complex than that. I believe that such groups are not representative of the spiritual patrimony or legacy of these religions. Judging by their actions, it is easy to see what lies beneath their religious ideology and sectarian rhetoric. Their agenda is criminal and destructive, especially as they target innocent lives and properties.

The key point here is that the abuse of religious sensibilities does not occur in a vacuum. When we look at Africa's flashpoints, there is evidence of underlying problems and root causes, all with significant political ramifications. Even before sectarian violence bubbles to the surface to become a major transnational challenge, there has existed and continues to exist severe political dysfunctionality that is compounded by economic and social collapse. The manifestations of this dysfunctionality are not hard to find. They include mismanagement of Africa's huge mineral and natural resources; kleptocratic and self-perpetuating regimes and political dynasties; and systemic corruption that consistently places the majority of African countries in the bottom half of Transparency International's "Corruption Perceptions Index."

Consider, for example, South Sudan, recently independent and one of the most fertile countries on the globe, boasting nine months of abundant rainfall. Since 2013 a ruinous civil war between an autocratic government and marauding bands of rebels and militias, each led by an egotistic opportunist, has reduced the country to a nation of famished refugees and internally displaced persons. The constitutive elements of this political dysfunctionality create a perfect storm for all kinds of ills, including sectarian violence. It is little wonder then that the extremists easily exploit such situations to make their cause attractive to millions of impoverished, disillusioned, and unemployed youth.

It would seem that what is often at stake in many conflicts in Africa is not necessarily faith or religious belief, but an instinct for survival and rebellion in the context of brutal socioeconomic and political conditions. This instinct increasingly mines the reserve of local grievances and is exacerbated by dehumanizing poverty and limited socioeconomic opportunities, leaving in its wake casualties of sectarian violence and religious intolerance.

Religion and Politics

In addition to blatant manifestations of sectarian violence, the realm of politics abounds with overt and covert signs of claims, contestations, and conflicts. Neither Christianity nor

Islam can be said to have intentionally and successfully integrated the principle of separation of religion and politics. Across Africa, politics remains one of the most fertile grounds for staking competing claims for supremacy by the continent's two dominant religions. Simply put, religion constitutes a significant factor of politics in Africa.

The example of Nigeria reveals some of the interesting dimensions of the fraught relationship between religion and politics in Africa. On one level, the tension between Christianity and Islam is played out in the political arena. Communities of either faith vigorously engage in political issues where and when each side feels threatened by the perceived or real ascendancy or dominance of the other. On occasion, this tension erupts in open violence between adherents of both religions. Similar to instances of terror groups masquerading as guardians of religious orthodoxy, the underlying issue here is the quest for power, which is a prerequisite for guaranteed access to immense economic resources. To forestall this kind of situation, a country like Tanzania has adopted an unofficial system of a rotating presidency, whereby the nation's top office is held alternately by a Christian and a Muslim.

The point I want to make here is that in many parts of Africa politics remains fertile ground for staking competing claims, carving out zones of influence, and pursuing vested interests by representatives and adherents of Christianity and Islam. Under these circumstances, any semblance of interreligious rapprochement is fraught with mutual suspicion. We can consider, for example, the patterns of major political events such as elections. Politicians are adept in courting religious leaders for votes; oftentimes, the latter are willing partners because they too curry the favor of politicians. This is not only divisive among denominations but also between religions. During constitutional changes in Kenya in 2010 Muslim leaders aligned themselves with politicians who publicly favored the establishment of Kadhi courts to adjudicate matters of family inheritance, marriage, and divorce among Muslim litigants. Unsurprisingly, Christian leaders joined cause with politicians who opposed the inclusion and validation of an Islamic legal system in the proposed constitution. Politics, not only ideology and beliefs, is a source of interreligious division and tension.

Across North Africa, most of the political systems draw on the tenets of Islam. Yet among them, whether in Egypt, Algeria, Morocco, Tunisia, or Libya, exist competing claims and diverse shades of interpretation of the relationship between Islam and politics and the legitimacy of political regimes as embodiments of Islamic traditions and practice. In the horn of Africa, the patent incursion of religion into politics in a country like Somalia is common knowledge in Africa's contemporary political history. Besides clan rivalries, religion remains a key factor in the failure of Somalia to organize itself and realize its potential as a viable modern state. Whether in Somalia, Sudan, Nigeria, Algeria, or Egypt, adherents do not mask their political agendas. For some adherents in these countries, the appropriation and direct control of the political establishment is considered a religious duty incumbent on every devout Muslim.

Below the Surface

Aside from the competing claims of Christianity and Islam in Africa, a different kind of conflict also rages on the religious landscape of the continent; I view this tension as a battle within the soul of the African. To establish a context to examine this phenomenon, I propose two hypotheses. The first probes the nature of religious conversion that I raised above, while the second focuses on the consequent conflict of religious heritage as it unfolds in the consciousness of the African.

As previously noted, the tripartite division of religious heritage in Africa is considered an axiom of religious scholarship. Instead, I directly challenge this underlying assumption of a tripartite taxonomy by arguing that African Religion is not one of three religious traditions but the *bedrock* on which Islam and Christianity are planted. In other words, I maintain that what religious scholarship designates as African Religion recognizes itself primarily as a way of life that is deeply embedded in the consciousness of people instead of being a religion in the same organized and reified sense in which Christianity and Islam are understood and studied as religions. I argue that what we call African Religion does not exist in parallel to the other two world religions as their correspondent or competitor. Africa does not experience a symmetrical relationship of three different religions. Rather, African Religion plays a key role in defining the *possibility* for the existence of Christianity and Islam within the same epistemological domain or religious consciousness. In other words, African Religion is the deep anchor that secures the foundation of either Christianity or Islam in the soul of the African. To the extent that either Christianity or Islam successfully maintains its vital moorings in this foundation or universe of meaning, it retains its relevance for Africans.

One consideration that has consistently eluded and frustrated theologians and social scientists is the realization that it is by virtue of their vital connection with the universe of meaning defined by African Religion that Christianity and Islam function at all within Africa's religious architecture. If we visualize African Religion as a foundation, both Christianity and Islam are steeples or minarets constructed upon this base. Seen in this light, it makes little sense to tout the numerical strength of Islam and Christianity as evidence of the decline or demise of African Religion.

The point, then, is this: African Religion does not seem to function side by side with Christianity and Islam, as is commonly presumed; rather, it operates below the layer of the competing claims and contestations of both religions. This explains in part the resilience of African Religion in the face of a sustained frontal assault by Christianity and Islam over the centuries. Using different imagery, I could liken the nature of African Religion to that of a dormant volcano in which this religious substratum erupts repeatedly into the consciousness and beliefs of the imported religions, but not in a violent manner. Thus the lava of African Religion runs deep in shaping the identities of Christians and Muslims alike.

It was Pope Paul VI who came closest to a formal endorsement of this insight in his message to the church of Africa (quoted in the first chapter) when he declared that "the African, who becomes a Christian, does not disown himself [or herself], but takes up the age-old values of tradition 'in spirit and in truth.'" Based on my personal experience, I maintain that this is how African Religion functions below the surface of the highly visible, claims, contestations, and conflicts of the organized and systematized faiths called Islam and Christianity.

One obvious implication ensues: If African Religion is the bedrock or substratum, as I am convinced it is, to what extent can religious conversion be considered a "coming to" or a "moving away from," as Isichei understands it? Does conversion not in fact imply a reshuffling of the religious deck to accommodate difference and moderate tension? Besides, to reiterate a point that I have made previously, African Religion is not missionary; its manifest objective does not include proselytization. By this singular virtue, analogically speaking, it is "ecumenically" receptive and "doctrinally" inclusive.

Many arguments can be advanced to demonstrate the validity of this hypothesis. The most obvious is any anecdotal and empirical evidence of attachment to beliefs and practices of African Religion by *converted* Christians and Muslims. As was pointed out in the study conducted by the Pew Forum, "traditional African religious beliefs and practices are common in predominantly Muslim countries, in countries with a more even mix of Christians and Muslims, and in predominantly Christian countries. . . . There is no clear pattern among Christians or Muslims on levels of engagement with African traditional religions."[11] When this study uses the innocuous term of "engagement," it denotes a real tension in the lives of African Christians and Muslims. Often, from their lack of understanding, some theologians have caricatured this tension variously and pejoratively as "faith schizophrenia" or "religious double-mindedness." Other uncomplimentary labels have also been employed.

Notwithstanding centuries of conversion, people who profess faith in Christianity or Islam still routinely participate in practices associated with African Religion: for example, consulting a diviner and/or healer in times of crisis; participating in ritual worship; and carrying or wearing objects or elements imbued with religious efficacy for the purposes of protection. If my hypothesis holds true, we have here a proverbial situation where you can take an African out of African Religion but cannot take African Religion out of an African. In his explanation of African conversion Robin Horton was wrong to suggest that removed from its microcosmic context so-called "African Traditional Religion" was of little or no use.[12] On the contrary, it is especially at moments of transition, liminality, and crisis occasioned by integration into the macrocosmic context that many Africans seek solace and support in the deep recesses of their ancestral religion.

Both Christianity and Islam have been quick to register their frustration at the tenuousness of religious allegiance, especially in times of crisis. This frustration would be mitigated by an understanding that under difficult circumstances "conversion" is a matter to be treated with hermeneutical circumspection. This is yet another reason why I caution against excessive fascination with the statistics of religious affiliation and conversion. Defining conversion exclusively by statistics offers a weak basis for stating Benedict's idea of the spiritual significance of Africa's religiosity for the rest of humanity.

The Dark Side of Light

To return to the question of competing claims, any glowing narratives of religious growth or vitality on the continent also contain a dark side. On account of past and recent events, but without overlooking the significant contributions of Christianity and Islam to healthcare and education, and charitable and emergency humanitarian assistance, for example, it can no longer be plausibly maintained that religion in Africa is always a force for good.

Nobel Peace laureate Wole Soyinka repeatedly indicted Christianity and Islam as "guilty not merely of physical atrocities on African soil, including enslavement of the indigenes, but of systematic assault on African spirituality in their contest for religious hegemony."[13] Judging by my experience of being labeled pejoratively by "Christians," this is a view with which I agree.

As recently as the abduction of 276 teenage schoolgirls in the town of Chibok in Nigeria in 2014 by Boko Haram; the brutal murder of 148 students, lecturers, and workers at Garissa University College in Kenya in 2015 by al-Shabaab; and the bloody siege of a hotel in Ouagadougou, Burkina Faso, in 2016 and 2017, by al-Qaeda in the Islamic Maghreb, event after event points to the escalating bellicosity of religiosity and the proliferation of sectarian cleavages in parts of the continent. With frightening intensity, these divisions have unleashed deadly religious and tribal passions in several areas of Africa, turning them into "a warring ground."[14]

However, it should be repeated that, whether in Kenya, Cameroon, Sudan, Tanzania, Egypt, Somalia, Mali, Burkina Faso, Tunisia, Nigeria, or Zanzibar, such ferocious proclivities that brutalize innocent humanity do not qualify as religion, no matter how stridently the chevaliers of religious separatism and theological irredentism declaim the righteousness of their cause, recruit and goad others into war, and sink their flag post deeper into the souls of Africans. Soyinka is right:

there is religion and there is fanaticism.[15] We may neither confuse nor conflate the two. What we are witnessing in Africa with increasing distress is the religious bigotry and mindless zealotry of what Soyinka calls "seasoned manipulators of irrational sentiment of faith"[16] and revelers "in the orgy of pietistic homicide"[17] These groups daily sharpen their blunt weapons of mass destruction at the clay feet of idols dressed as supreme deities. Unsurprisingly, when these "deities are co-opted to lend authority to human sentiments and proclivities, humanity becomes disposable to usurpers of divine authority and custodians of mere dogma."[18]

However, this assessment of religious violence in Africa would be biased if it focuses exclusively on Kalashnikov-waving zealots clad in suicide vests as the sole perpetrators of sectarian intolerance. Emeritus Archbishop of Canterbury Rowan Williams has described an extremist as "someone who has simply fixed on a moment in the living tradition and frozen it."[19] As I suggested in the previous chapter, there is another form of extremism and fundamentalism orchestrated by those on the continent who operate a kind of religious economy that preys on the gullibility and disillusionment of desperate Africans. With entrepreneurial sophistication and cunning, jet-setting preachers and their army of evangelical clones have devised a brand of Christianity that spiritualizes Africa's real and deadly challenges. The danger is that such a tendency toward spiritualization trivializes religion and makes it into an instrument for pursuing self-serving interests and achieving personal gains. With evangelical certitude, agents of this religious phenomenon proceed to strip concrete economic, social, and political challenges of any real substance, while simultaneously attributing their causes to a personal failing or ancestral malediction or by presenting dubious options as the panacea for all of the continent's crises. In the bogus exegesis of this sophisticated spiritual diagnosis, the cost of deliverance, healing, or salvation is a dose of faith heavily coated with lavish monetary offerings to Africa's merchants of a prosperity gospel.[20]

If Benedict XVI has correctly described Africa as the lung of humanity, religious zealotry and evangelical bigotry connive today to asphyxiate this lung. Happily, as I am keen to point out, this is not the end of the story of the function of religion in Africa. As an African proverb says, when a child is chastised by his or her father, he or she seeks refuge in his or her mother's hut. The tension and abuse orchestrated by elements within Christianity and Islam allow us to explore other options for a more meaningful understanding and practice of religion. In other words, the experience of religious claims, contestations, and conflicts offers an impetus to discover and consider seriously African Religion as a source of spiritual revivification, albeit one that has consistently been dismissed and combated by Christianity and Islam.

The Spirit of African Religion

As I have experienced it, African Religion stands as a crucial, if somewhat misunderstood and vilified, bulwark against extremist attempts to dissolve the essence and value of religion in an orgy of sectarian ideology and hypocrisy. Liberated from the zero-sum game of mutually assured destruction that characterizes Africa's two dominant religions in some places, the spirit of African Religion is a vital repository of humanity that can sustain belief in the future of religion on the continent and that can school its people in the art of dignified coexistence. If this were not the case, why do Africans time and again resort to agents of their ancestral way of life, even though they are routinely castigated as witchdoctors, for guidance and relief?

A term that is shorthand for the conceptualization of the core of African Religion is the notion of *ubuntu*, a Bantu term of southern Africa popularized by Anglican Archbishop Desmond Tutu. In its unencumbered sense, *ubuntu* is a simple idea that prioritizes inclusivity over exclusivity, community over competition, hospitality over hostility, dialogue over confrontation and respect over domination: "[U]*buntu* means we cannot turn our backs on anyone who genuinely wants to be part of our community. . . . *Ubuntu* in this sense places dialogue at the center of what it means to be fully human. It involves a future that seeks to rise above exclusion and alienation."[21] Curiously, in their essence, both Christianity and Islam lay claims to this ideal of inclusive and egalitarian community; in practice, however, as I have demonstrated, such claims are increasingly weakened by sectarian tendencies.

Without intending to canonize this religious tradition, perhaps, then, the gift of African Religion to the world lies in its deep wells of humanizing values *alive and active in the spirit of African Christians and Muslims* and not in any hubris of sectarianism and extremism. Devoid of pretensions to power and proselytizing strategies, an African spiritual consciousness "is peculiarly concerned with the aspiration to be human in a particular form and, therefore, with living satisfactory and responsible lives, both singular and in common, reflectively and actively."[22] If this aspiration and practice is what was harshly—and continues to be—labeled as animism, then I do not regret claiming it as my heritage and tradition.

If this is so, Benedict stands vindicated, for the authentic spirituality of this continent is a profound repository of resources for the renewal of humanity. The world and Africa stand in dire need of a commitment to safeguard the spirit of tolerance and inclusivity that characterizes African Religion as a global heritage. For, as Soyinka has argued, "[I]f Africa falls to the will of the [religious] fanatic, then the insecurity of the world should be accepted as its future and permanent condition. There are no other options."[23]

To reiterate an important point, although historians and scholars of religions usually filter the continent's contemporary religious identity through a triple heritage of African Traditional Religion, Christianity, and Islam, I maintain that the first of these sits rather uncomfortably within this classification. Indeed, it is the *ground* or *bedrock* on which the other two stake their claims to the African soul, evidenced by the fact that, in various parts of the continent, people are at ease with mixing and matching elements of these faith traditions. I witnessed such exercises at my father's bedside prayer sessions. I choose to interpret what others have derided as syncretistic proclivity as a healthy form of religious coexistence and tolerance, and therefore a resource in an era of violent and destructive fundamentalism, sectarianism, and extremism.

Notwithstanding this positive interpretation, we cannot dismiss the reality of the multiple layers of tension among these religious traditions in Africa, examples and signs of which are not hard to find in the ongoing crises in several African countries. They pose a real challenge to the task of interreligious dialogue and ecumenism in Africa and elsewhere. Yet the spirit of hospitality and tolerance that imbues African spirituality with its unique character can be a resource for global religious traditions in their quest for dialogue, tolerance, and mutuality as modes of coexistence, creating a context of religious pluralism and diversity.

Let me end the way I began this chapter with a fitting anecdote that doubles as an antidote. In December 2015, a group of al-Shabaab militants attacked a busload of travellers in the Mandera region of northeastern Kenya. As customary in their macabre rituals, the attackers proceeded to separate Christians from Muslims, intending to slaughter the former and spare the latter. A Muslim teacher, Salah Farah, refused to obey orders to segregate people on the basis of their religious affiliation. For his dissent he was shot and critically wounded. Fighting for his life in a hospital bed in Nairobi, Farah recounted the event and explained the rationale for his action:

> They told us if you are a Muslim, we are safe. . . . We asked them to kill all of us or leave us alone. . . . We are brothers. People should live peacefully together. . . . It's only the religion that is the difference, so I ask my brother Muslims to take care of the Christians so that the Christians also take care of us . . . and let us help one another and let us live together peacefully.[24]

On Monday, January 18, 2016, Farah died in surgery to treat his bullet wound, his life a potent antidote to the lethal religious claims, contestations, and conflicts in Africa and in the world.

Notes

1. Emmanuel Katongole, "The Church of the Future: Pressing Moral Issues from Ecclesia in Africa," in *The Church We Want: African Catholics Look to Vatican III*, ed. Agbonkhianmeghe E. Orobator (Maryknoll, NY: Orbis Books, 2106), 168.

2. http://www.vatican.va/holy_father/benedict_xvi/homilies/2009/documents/hf_ben-xvi_hom_20091004_sinodo-africa_en.html.

3. Laurenti Magesa, *African Religion: The Moral Traditions of Abundant Life* (Maryknoll, NY: Orbis Books, 1997), 14–18.

4. Ibid., 18–28.

5. W. Montgomery Watt, *Muhammad: Prophet and Statesman* (Oxford: Oxford University Press, 1961).

6. The Pew Forum on Religion and Public Life, "Tolerance and Tension: Islam and Christianity in Sub–Saharan Africa" (http://www.pewforum.org/2010/04/15/executive-summary-islam-and-chrisitianity-in-sub-saharan-africa/).

7. Ibid.

8. Elizabeth Isichei, *The Religious Traditions of Africa: A History* (Westport, CT: Praeger, 2004), 4.

9. China Achebe, *Things Fall Apart* (New York: Anchor Books, 1994), 140–41.

10. Ibid., 155.

11. The Pew Forum on Religion and Public Life, "Tolerance and Tension."

12. See Robert Horton, "African Conversion," *Africa* 41 (1971): 85–108; "On the Rationality of Conversion (Part 1)," *Africa* 45 (1975): 219–35; "On the Rationality of Conversion (Part 2)," *Africa* 45 (1975): 373–99.

13. Wole Soyinka, *Of Africa* (New Haven and London: Yale University Press, 2012), xi.

14. Ibid, 129.

15. Ibid.

16. Ibid, 141.

17. Ibid, 197.

18. Ibid, 198.

19. Rowan Williams, *Faith in the Public Square* (London: Bloomsbury, 2012), 83.

20. See John L. Allen, Jr., *The Future Church: How Ten Trends Are Revolutionizing the Catholic Church* (New York: Doubleday, 2009), 438; Paul Gifford, *African Christianity: Its Public Role* (Bloomington, IN: Indiana University Press, 1998), 39–40.

21. Gabriel Setiloane, quoted in Charles Villa-Vincencio, *Walk with Us and Listen: Political Reconciliation in Africa* (Washington, DC: Georgetown University Press, 2009), 113; see also Cedric Mayson, *Why Africa Matters* (Maryknoll, NY: Orbis Books, 2010), 31–33.

22. Timothy Jenkins, *Religion in English Everyday Life: An Ethnographic Approach* (New York: Berghahn Books, 1999), 14.

23. Soyinka, *Of Africa*, 130.

24. http://www.bbc.co.uk.news/world-africa-35352763.

4

Pathological Performance and Prophetic Practice

In a continent full of bad news, how is the Christian message "Good News" for our people? In the midst of an all-pervading despair, where lies the hope and optimism which the Gospel brings?

—*Cardinal Hyacinthe Thiandoum*

On March 17, 2000, five hundred men, women, and children perished in a massive inferno in the rural village of Kanungu in southwestern Uganda. The victims were members of a Christian religious group known as the Movement for the Restoration of the Ten Commandments of God. Investigation led to the discovery of more mass graves in and around the capital city, Kampala, linked to the massacre, bringing the tally of casualties to close to 1,000 dead. Although unconfirmed, by this count, the Kanungu massacre exceeded the casualty figure of the Jonestown (Guyana) tragedy in 1978, and counts as the deadliest single massacre orchestrated by a Christian sect. Needless to say, the leaders of the movement claimed religious inspiration for their particular style of Christian beliefs and behavior.[1]

77

On 16 April, 2015, police and defence forces killed scores of members of a Christian sect known as the Seventh Day in the Light of the World in Angola's central highlands of Huambo, to avenge the death of eight police officers, allegedly at the hands of sect members. Several police officers were killed as they attempted to arrest the sect leader, José Kalupeteka, during worship. The sect is an offshoot of the Seventh-Day Adventist Church. More than 3,000 followers from many parts of the country had camped at Mount Sumi, in Huambo province, for the sect's summit. Mr Kalupeteka preached that the world will end in December 2015, and urged followers to abandon all their belongings and live in seclusion, while awaiting the end of the world.[2]

Macabre stories like these underline a propensity for certain brands of religiosity to degenerate into extreme pathological situations. While not all pathologies of religious performance manifest such devastating consequences as in Kanungu and Mount Sumi, the fact remains that a certain perversion of Christianity in Africa forms part of the narrative of religious expansion and growth on the continent.

Increasingly sensational manifestations of Christian beliefs and practices can caricature the authentic tenets of the faith, at best, or pervert its core values, at worst. A variety of media platforms and channels are replete with implausible news of exhibitionist evangelism—such as a preacher who communicates directly with God via a cell phone; a purported healer and spirit medium who draws diesel fuel from a rock (à la Moses in the desert); a self-styled prophet curing diseases with insecticide; or a pastor egging on his congregation to indulge in eating live snakes. The list of bizarre claims purportedly anchored on Christian beliefs in Africa is as long as the foundation of these claims is flimsy. Africa is no exception in this regard; pathologies of religious performance exist all over the world.

In the preceding chapters, I have argued that religious expansion is not simply a function of numerical or statistical considerations. Any critical assessment of the practice, outcomes, and impact of religious growth anywhere needs to take into account a wider set of factors. Read exclusively in statistical terms, expansion of religion in Africa, as elsewhere, risks masking its pathological dimension. Thus, I want to look more closely and critically at the practice, outcomes, and impact of Christianity in Africa, describing some of the uses and abuses of religion, in this case, Christianity.

Three points are particularly relevant to situate and frame the assumptions that underlie my intent. First, my choice of the terms "pathology" and "abuse" is intentional. Granted, they may seem unduly harsh labels for examining the functioning of Christianity in Africa, but African Religion has been labeled with harsher terms. These terms translate in part my intent to critique the direction and orientation of religious affiliation and allegiance in Africa today. As I mentioned earlier, there is nothing definitive or absolute about my approach. I take a very personal view. In fact, I welcome a further critique in order, as much as possible, to build a comprehensive and accurate narrative of what faith and religion mean and how they function—how they are used and abused in Africa.

Second, my critique is heavily influenced by my dual heritage. As should be clear by now, although I am a convert to Catholic Christianity, I continue to draw significant inspiration from my background in African Religion. This dual religious identity accounts for certain biases that may filter my narrative. I have made, however, an effort to ensure that they do not diminish its pertinence in my attempt to understand the intricacies and complexities of religious allegiance and affiliation in Africa.

More than forty years ago, the English social anthropologist and philosopher Robin Horton, whom I briefly introduced in chapters 2 and 3, argued that a typical cosmology of religious traditions like African Religion comprises "a system of ideas about unobservable personal beings whose activities are alleged to underpin the events of the ordinary, everyday world. . . ."[3] More importantly, Horton claimed, this cosmology performs a triple function: "It provides an impressive instrument for explanation, prediction and control."[4] Thus, this system or cosmology that comprises a phalanx of spiritual entities and forces, attempting to tame or neutralize malevolent ones and harness the positive energy in the benevolent ones, is highly functional, utilitarian, and, inevitably, prone to manipulation and exploitation.

Paul Gifford, who also subscribes to Horton's position, has christened this system an "enchanted religious imagination."[5] Gifford claims that this system is pervasive and persistent in African religiosity of Christian extraction. As I explained in the previous chapter, this religious imagination continues to inform and shape the attitudes of Africans, even after conversion to Christianity or Islam. The pervasive and persistent phenomenon described by Gifford confirms the observation of sociologist Birgit Meyer, who conducted an extensive empirical study in West Africa, that "so-called 'traditional' religion is not something of the past (although Christian rhetoric locates it there), but is still practiced and, as it seems, on the increase."[6] The continued influence of African Religion in daily life is corroborated by the 2010 scientific report published by the Pew Forum. According to the report:

> Side by side with their high levels of commitment to Christianity and Islam, many people in the countries surveyed retain beliefs and rituals that are characteristic of traditional African religions. In four countries, for instance, half or more of the population believes that sacrifices to ancestors or spirits can protect them from harm. In addition, roughly a quarter or more of the population in 11 countries say they believe in the protective power

of juju (charms or amulets), shrines and other sacred objects. Belief in the power of such objects is highest in Senegal (75%) and lowest in Rwanda (5%).[7]

It is not surprising, then, that several brands of African Christianity have appropriated African Religion's characteristic functions of explanation, prediction, and control. In this sense, I hold that they too could justly be considered varieties of "enchanted" Christianity. Manifestations of such religious imagination are widespread in Africa, particularly among churches of Pentecostal extraction, which Gifford labels "African Pentecostalism." It is important to bear in mind that in this enchanted world religion serves a purpose and can indeed be pressed into service in a variety of situations, conditions, or circumstances. Only a thin line demarcates a pervasive system of religious practice from a perverted system of religious performance. This leads to my third point.

To describe and evaluate the uses and abuses of Christianity, I adopt the dual category of *prophetic practice* and *pathological performance*. This distinction is subtle but functional as a hermeneutical tool. Manifestations of *prophetic practice* exemplify and embody the authentic meaning and purpose of Christianity. *Pathological performance*, to the contrary, constitutes a subversion or perversion of Christianity's authentic meaning and purpose. Anecdotes such as those at the beginning of this chapter serve as practical examples.

The reader may rightly object and question my rationale for making such a judgment on what is authentic and what is not. I shoulder my burden of subjectivity and hope that the authenticity of purpose and meaning as regards Christianity is more self-evident than it would seem at first thought. Also, in speaking of prophetic practice versus pathological performance in Christianity, I have noted the tendency to generalize about the African continent. As much as it is possible, I make a conscious effort to identify particular instances that illustrate and justify some general statements about religious affiliation and allegiance in Africa. The temptation to reduce Africa to a simple and homogenous entity—what Nigerian writer Chimamanda Ngozi Adichie calls "a single story"—remains the bane of research and scholarship across several disciplines that focus on the continent. I plead no exception.

The Ghost and the Darkness

As should be evident by now, the religious scenario in Africa in the twenty-first century, especially south of the Sahara, confronts us with a fascinating though perplexing panorama in several ways. The first striking example relates to the strong evidence of growth and expansion of religious affiliation and allegiance. Abundant documentation of this phenomenon of surging growth exists in studies of history, sociology, religion, and theology. As already noted, the axis of religious growth and expansion has risen steeply since the turn of the twentieth century. Stemming from the incursion of missionary Christianity into Africa in the eighteenth and nineteenth centuries, Christianity has gradually, steadily, and strongly registered its presence on the continental map as a major religion. The same is true of Islam, since its advent in North Africa in the seventh century.

A second element of fascination and perplexity concerns categorization. What constitutes an accurate taxonomy of religion in Africa? Desirable as it would seem, reality consistently thwarts the best-laid methodologies. Christianity south of the Sahara, with its proliferation of movements, sects, and churches, can appear bewildering. In chapter 2, I observed that, according to Lamin Sanneh, the preponderant factor that accounts for this religious diversity and intense growth is a process known as translation and vernacularization.

As more and more Africans are able to access translations of the Bible in their vernacular language, they gain confidence in appropriating its message and are empowered then to produce their own "brands" or "expressions" of Christianity. Using selectivity and creativity they begin to translate Christianity itself into their local context. However, vernacularization generally foils any attempt to foist lasting regulatory canons on the formation of Christian churches and communities. In other words, vernacularization triggers a liberalization that in turn promotes a proliferation of myriad Christian bodies. The result is a complex diversity of ecclesial communities. In Africa, while it is still possible to talk about mainline churches, such as the Roman Catholic, Anglican, Methodist, and Presbyterian churches, for example, the vast majority of ecclesial units defy easy categorization or classification.

As a consequence, the "standard" labels of faith traditions at our disposal no longer capture and represent the defining characteristics of these incessantly evolving and mutating ecclesial units. The persistent fluidity inherent in their nature, identity, theology, and beliefs thwarts any neat, fixed, and static categorization. Presently, the terms Pentecostal, evangelical, Protestant, charismatic, Zionist, instituted, Ethiopic, independent, and so on embody a frustrating relativity that almost neutralizes their relevance as denominational boundary markers. Other tags like "Bible-believing," "miracle-working," "deliverance," "white-garment," "Spirit-filled," "prophetic," "anointed," and "end-time" fare no better. As the Christian message and its beliefs are legitimately translatable into local and practical vernaculars, so also are they extremely prone to manipulation by religious con artists.

The sum of these preliminary remarks is simply and surprisingly that, however we view it, religion is doing well in Africa. But the question that I raise is equally as simple: *How should we view religion in Africa?* As I have already pointed out, the dominant approach tends to focus substantially and disproportionately on demographics and statistics. Consider, therefore, the two following examples.

Philip Jenkins is convinced that the new faces of Christianity emerging in the geographical and demographic spheres of

Africa, Asia, and Latin America constitute the next Christendom.[8] When we probe the rationale behind this projection, numbers surface as key factors and considerations.

Similarly, John Allen, Jr., is convinced that a shift of the center of gravity to the global South is one of the significant trends that will revolutionize the future Catholic Church. Like Jenkins, he argues that Latin America, Asia, and Africa will lead the church, albeit in the direction of social conservatism and evangelical Pentecostalism.[9]

I do not dispute the importance of the demographics and statistics that characterize their approaches. The numbers and statistics are justly qualified as staggering. An important caution, nonetheless, is the temptation or risk of absolutizing numbers to the detriment of incisive analysis and probing critique of the trends, credibility, and authenticity of religious affiliation and allegiance in Africa. The narrative of growth in religion in Africa has good sides and not-so-good sides; both Jenkins and Allen also acknowledge this.[10]

A Religion of Underdevelopment

Notwithstanding its statistical success, when set in the wider horizon of Africa, the growth of Christianity and other religions throws up a sharp and disconcerting image. Ironically, the continent's economic and political fortunes seem to regress in inverse proportion to the prospects of Christianity. There is little need for statistics to portray the current economic, social, and political predicament of the continent. The evidence leans heavily in the direction of deterioration rather than amelioration. It is debatable whether one should qualify the situation as hopeless or hopeful. Such ambivalence was aptly captured in the journalistic about-turn of *The Economist* magazine that labeled Africa "the hopeless continent" at the turn of the millennium, hailed it as "Africa rising" in 2011, and rechristened it "a hopeful continent" in 2013.[11]

Another important question concerning religion in Africa is why religion flourishes on a continent suffused with crises, calamities, and conflicts? Why does religion thrive in the midst of underdevelopment and widespread dysfunctionality? Notable attempts have been made to confront these questions and to critique religion in Africa. Paul Gifford has undertaken extensive empirical studies of Christian denominations in Africa, especially in West and East Africa. His studies offer useful insights on the trends and characteristics of Christianity in Africa in the late twentieth century and the early twenty-first century.[12]

Another pertinent example is Ugandan theologian Emmanuel Katongole, whom I introduced in chapter 2. In his aptly titled book, *The Sacrifice of Africa*, Katongole argues that Christianity operates within an essentially questionable paradigm—limited at best, flawed at worst. Whereas Christian performance concentrates on applying soothing spiritual, pastoral, and political salves to complex and complicated socioeconomic and political challenges, it fails to impact the course or direction of these domains in any significant manner. Katongole wonders: "What accounts for the dismal social impact of Christianity in Africa? Why has Christianity, despite its overwhelming presence, failed to make a significant dent in the social history of the continent?"[13] This question is certainly of interest for a continent renowned for an explosion of religious growth. Katongole's preferred solution consists of a reimagination of Christianity's core values as social ethics and the creation of new narratives that overcome Christianity's reticence as a social imaginary in order to generate effective alternatives and solutions.

The difference that I find between Gifford and Katongole is that while Gifford limits his analysis mostly to empirical accounts, Katongole offers theological considerations and rationale. This is not surprising considering that Gifford approaches the issue from his perspective as a sociologist of religion, while Katongole does not disguise his theological bent. The general conclusion of Gifford is an indictment of churches and religious institutions for their failure to contribute to the "radical restructuring" of Africa's socioeconomic and political institutions.[14]

So why is religion doing so well in the midst of crisis in Africa? I propose to reformulate the question, primarily because the challenge is not to come up with a conceptual evaluation or assessment. Rather, the challenge is to rethink the relevance of religion in Africa in the twenty-first century. I now propose a third question *"Why does religion work in Africa?"* in addition to the earlier questions of "How do we view religion?" and "Why does religion thrive in the midst of chaos and dislocation?" The underpinning of this third question derives from observing religious phenomena in Africa: religion works. This is as true for Christianity and Islam as it is for African Religion. And there is an intensity of affiliation and allegiance in the way religion works. Formal doctrinal and dogmatic concerns seem to matter less than practical and functional benefits of faith and belief.

Religion Works

Religion works. When we pay close attention to the structure of belief in African Religion we see there is a category of deities that hold sway over the allegiance of adherents exclusively because of their functionality. Anthropologists have generally labeled these deities as "lesser gods" and juxtaposed them with "the Supreme Being." This distinction explains the religious behavior of my father that I described in the first chapter on the faith of my father and the spirit of my mother.

Many scholars of African Religion still argue that what is characterized as Supreme Being is rendered otiose and distant by the fact that there are rarely any cults, devotees, or shrines affiliated with it. They maintain that because of this distancing or remoteness, Africans have tended to create a panoply of "lesser agents, the gods, and spirits," to deal with "the fortunes and misfortunes of everyday life."[15] Instead, I argue that to label these as "secondary," "economic," or "lesser" gods, as some scholars like Dominique Zahan and Benjamin C. Ray have done, is to miss the point. From the point of view of the devotees there is nothing secondary or economic about these gods and spirits. They are important because they are believed and perceived to work in the interest of their devotees in a variety of situations, especially at times of crisis, such as illness, threat of failure, survival, annihilation, and so on. When members of my extended family drew water from the medicine room we believed not only in the efficacy of the elements, but more importantly in the potent guarantee of the deities.

In chapter 1 I mentioned the case of Chief Akunna and the missionary, Mr. Brown, where the chief stated in clear terms the nature of the so-called "lesser" gods and goddesses as "messengers." They neither compete with nor replace the Supreme Being, and they certainly do not render the Supreme Being meaningless. Each has its place. Ray is correct to note that "both types of divinity, the One Creator God and the many lesser powers are essential to the full range of traditional religious experience."[16] Failure to comprehend this relationship explains in part the label and burden of "animism" that missionary Christianity foisted on African Religion. In this sense, I hold the position that they too could justly be considered varieties of "enchanted Christianity." Religion does work in Africa. I concur with Paul Gifford that Christianity in Africa has adopted and adapted this functional and utilitarian mindset that characterizes the structure of religious allegiance and belief in contemporary Africa, something that Gifford calls the "enchanted religious imagination."

To gain a better understanding of how religion currently works in Africa, it is important to recall the two modes of functionality that I introduced above: pathological performance and prophetic practice. This classification also takes into account the interconnected questions of how we view religion in Africa and why religion is doing so well in Africa despite the evidence of widespread socioeconomic and political dysfunctionality.

Pathological Performance

In general, any pathological performance of religion manipulates and appropriates religious resources and language to generate simple and superficial solutions to real and complex problems or challenges. Such performance usually capitalizes on the superficial aspects of religion and enhances the perception of their efficacy in the eyes and minds of adherents. It makes use of a simplistic theology and hermeneutics, and it co-opts multiple communication strategies to amplify such perceptions. Common and obvious strategies include, for example, media technology, marketing gimmicks, self-publication, and advertising techniques. Pope Francis has described such pseudo-evangelical pyrotechnics as "a means of exploiting the weaknesses of people living in poverty and on the fringes of society, people who make ends meet amid great human suffering and are looking for immediate solutions to their needs" (*Evangelii Gaudium* [Joy of the Gospel], 63). However we look at it, religious performance, as I use the term, is a distortion and a diversion.

I do not claim any methodological copyright over the term *performance*. "Performance" is common currency in the description of phenomena and actions across many social science disciplines. Laurenti Magesa, for example, describes performance in relation to African spirituality as "an artistic feat toward the discovery of beauty, which involves the process of both learning and producing meaning and constructing cultural norms and social identities."[17] For the sake of the present narrative, I qualify performance with "pathology," precisely to highlight those *disturbing dimensions* of Christianity as it operates in Africa in the twenty-first century.

Christianity south of the Sahara exhibits three interesting platforms where the practice of religion operates as performance and is prone to pathological manifestations:

- *Healing*, in particular, miraculous healing;
- *Prophecy*/visions, relating to the material wellbeing, conditions, and misfortunes/fortunes of adherents; and
- *Deliverance*, the need to neutralize and eliminate forces that are perceived to stand in the way of the socioeconomic advancement of an adherent.

Together all three platforms replicate—or, at least, mirror—Horton's tripartite framework of explanation, prediction, and control prevalent in African Religion.

Noticeably absent from this framework is the much-debated gospel of prosperity. In its simplest form, this "gospel" prioritizes material prosperity and success as divine recompense for faith, while abhorring poverty as the assigned lot of people of little or no faith. The dividing line between both is best explained by the pecuniary interest attached to the former. The gospel of prosperity, which I will take up later, can be subsumed under any of the three platforms.

Although the focus at present is on Christianity, pathologies of religion operate in other religions as well. We could, for example, think of elements within Islam that foment psychological intimidation and physical and material violence. I described some of these pathological examples of Islam in chapter 3. Yet it is important to concede that such elements are motivated by factors that are not necessarily derived from the core values or tenets of Islam. In both Christianity and Islam, pathological performance is further complicated and emboldened by growing religious intolerance, the instrumentalization of religious allegiance, the commercialization of religious consciousness, and an intensification of religious extremism.

There are numerous unflattering specimens of pathological performance. The studies of Gifford include many accounts of pathological performance associated with Christianity in Africa. Some descriptions are particularly arresting, if not downright frightening. Consider the case of Daniel Olukoya, the founder of Mountain of Fire and Miracle Ministries. The name of this group, like others, should already give pause. According to Gifford, this group is an example of African Pentecostalism "pushed to its limits."[18] Olukoya teaches that a Christian is perpetually subjected to the threat of ubiquitous and malevolent spiritual forces that include ancestral curses, marine spirits, serpent spirits, occult spouses, and witches. These forces hold hapless Christians in permanent spiritual bondage. The price of freedom is a combination of repentance, righteousness, deliverance, and prayer. As Gifford comments:

> What essentially characterizes Olukoya's Christianity is spiritual warfare. . . . The essence of his Christianity is prayer—violent prayers, "holy madness," the "offensive warfare" of a "firebrand warrior"—either in church or at home. This prayer is the principal means of thwarting the evil forces arrayed against us and reclaiming our true destiny. . . .[19]

If the belligerency of Olukoya's firebrand Christianity unsettles rationality, other examples defy credulity.

Consider an event that gained national notoriety in the West African country of Ghana. When the national currency, the *cedi*, suddenly took a nosedive and lost value against all major foreign currencies, the event understandably sent shock waves across the nation's economy and triggered a catastrophic inflationary reaction. In the ensuing generalized panic, one prominent Ghanaian Christian leader invented "a Christian" solution to the monetary crisis of a rapidly depreciating *cedi*. Archbishop Nicholas Duncan-Williams, presiding bishop of the Christian Action Faith Ministries (CAFM), Action Chapel, attributed the problem to the work of Satan. The following is his deliverance prayer to reverse the satanic calamity of currency depreciation and to decree "the resurrection of the cedi":

> In the name of Jesus, I say Satan take your hands off the President; take your hands off the Central Bank and the Finance Minister. We release innovation for the President, my God, the Governor of the Central Bank of Ghana. . . . We command new ideas, breakthroughs and a miracle for the economy. Let the Cedi rise in Jesus' name! . . . I hold up the Cedi with prayer and I command the Cedi to recover and I declare the Cedi will not fall. It will not fall any further. I command the Cedi to climb. I command the resurrection of the Cedi. I command and release a miracle for the economy!

Theatrics apart, some reactions to such religious antics justly recognize them for what they are. A case in point is the reaction of the former head of Ghana's Monitoring and Evaluation of the National Democratic Congress (NDC) administration, Dr. Tony Aidoo. In his comments on the bishop's antics, he observes that:

> At best, it is a comic relief, but seriously, at worst, it is a big problem for us because it goes to reinforce the attitude—the undevelopmental attitude of Ghanaians. . . . You attribute everything that is positive to God and everything that is negative to the devil, so the two names become the most . . . commercialized. And then you become vulnerable to the exploitation of the clergy.[20]

Under such circumstances, the greatest threat that such a religious pathological performance poses to Africa lies in the singular ability of its proponents to create and reinforce a dualistic hermeneutical framework that opposes good and evil. It also produces a reductionist theology that spiritualizes all forms of socioeconomic malaise, in both private and public domains.

As noted before, Gifford describes this penchant for the spiritualization of all aspects of life as an "enchanted worldview" that "sees spiritual causality everywhere."[21] Although I agree with Gifford's nomenclature and observation, I dispute his tendency to locate the origin of this enchanted worldview exclusively within African beliefs or what he pejoratively brands witchcraft. As I have consistently maintained, although there is evidence of influence, African Religion does not account entirely for the rise and perpetuation of such pathological performances. Besides, African Religion does not countenance witchcraft; it considers it an aberration.

Similarly, I disagree with Jenkins's characterization of this proclivity for spiritual causality as simply "pagan inheritance" or the "continuing influence of pagan and animistic beliefs" on African Christianity.[22] The African gods and goddesses are not to blame. This enchanted worldview for the purposes of financial and pecuniary interests is primarily an invention and a potent instrument of the peddlers of such pathological performances. As Aidoo perceptively notes, the principal tools of pathological performance are exploitation and manipulation.[23]

Essentially, however, any pathological performance is a by-product of a flawed Christology generated by reductionist thinking. Having juxtaposed good and evil, it reduces the function, role, or meaning of the entire teaching, mission, and gospel of Christ to a weapon for opposing, taming, neutralizing, and defeating evil incarnated in a coterie of malevolent spirits. Besides, it lays undue stress on the functionality of this gospel to procure everything that it presupposes is denied or opposed by evil spirits—essentially prosperity, in the form of wealth and health. Accordingly, Jesus Christ becomes primarily and exclusively the prized purveyor of material prosperity and the great guarantor of victory against the ubiquitous and marauding spirits.

It is customary for this "enchanted" Christianity to compare the power of Christ with the power of Satan and evil spirits. A popular song portrays Jesus' power as "superpower" and Satan's power as "powerless power." Within such a simple binary conceptualization, Jesus Christ can be pressed into service in any variety of situations perceived as threatening.

As is evident in the foregoing, there is no dearth of examples of pathological performance from the ludicrous to the dangerous. It is worth noting that besides their financial interests, many of its proponents or entrepreneurs eventually succeed in wielding significant political influence. As one analyst has described them, "Africa's latter-day self-styled prophets . . . head mega churches with flocks running into millions. They preach but also mingle with politicians. They have a certain mystique and are revered by many. When they talk, even leaders listen."[24]

Such religious entrepreneurs play incessantly to the gallery of Africa's cast of megalomaniacs, autocrats, dictators, and despots. Prophet T. B. Joshua is legendary for the number of Africa's late, former, and serving presidents or heads of states listed in his fan base. The list includes the late Frederick Chiluba of Zambia, the late John Atta Mills of Ghana, the late Bingu wa Mutharika of Malawi, former president Joyce Banda of Malawi (whose predecessor's death Prophet Joshua claimed he predicted), former Zimbabwean Prime Minister Morgan Tsvangirai. His SCOAN website describes him as "a mentor to presidents yet a friend to the widows and less privileged, a role model to his generation yet a humble and hardworking man, toiling tirelessly for the advancement of God's kingdom."

Another tragic example of pathological performance is the case of the self-proclaimed Congolese prophet Joseph Mukungubila Mutombo, also known as "God's last envoy to humanity after Jesus Christ and Paul of Tarsus." In 2013, Mutombo led a band of followers in a spate of audacious deadly attacks on government and security installations in the Democratic Republic of Congo. The incident resulted in the death of scores of followers and security operatives.

Notwithstanding these manifestations and its questionable Christological credentials, pathological performance exemplifies a "weak religion," a religion that at its best, is diversionary and misleading, and at its worst, manipulative and exploitative.

R. Scott Appleby has studied the triple phenomenon of "strong," "weak," and "pathological" religions in exploring the complex relationship between religion and violence. To put it simply, there is religion and there is violence. Given certain conditions or circumstances, or in a given context, the former can trigger and even proffer rationale for the latter.[25] However, when I speak of "weak religion," I do not contrast it with "strong religion" or invest it with the meaning of failure to mobilize the resources of religion for a sustained political action in the public sphere—which is similar to Katongole's position. To my mind, pathological religious performance is weak religion to the degree that a sophisticated and messianic cohort of opportunists and charlatans exploits the innocence of adherents for narrow economic ends and self-serving political agendas. By doing so, they attenuate and dilute the transformative potential of religious faith. To quote Karl Maier, who has studied this phenomenon in Nigeria, "These modern-day pastors are simply preying upon the gullibility of their wealthier adherents and the desperation of the poor."[26] No more, no less.

Along similar lines, Paul Gifford proposes and defends the idea that pathological performance leads to a domestication of Christianity, by which he means that, in the case of Kenya, for example, "Christianity has become an integral part of the dysfunctional system."[27] It raises the question whether such performance can still be categorized as "Christian."

What I consider more illuminating is Appleby's notion of *ambivalence*. The internal structure and material resources of religion can serve dual and multiple purposes depending on the controlling agent or the overarching ideological and doctrinal proclivities of its protagonists. In other words, given its ambivalence and the internal plurality of interpretations, religion can function as performance and as practice, pathologically in the former, and prophetically in the latter.[28]

Prophetic Practice

So far, not much consideration has been given to the second way that religion currently works in Africa, although I have alluded extensively to it. Because my focus so far has been on the strategies and manifestations of pathological religious performance, now I must offer a similar account of "prophetic practice," rather than presume its self-evident properties.

Drawing on my own experience of African Religion, religious practice is essentially oriented toward enhancing and strengthening life broadly conceived. Whether in ritual, worship, or divination, the primary benefit of religious allegiance is derived from the belief that such practice enhances the life-force of devotees individually and collectively. It would be disingenuous to deny that there are no aberrations—as with pathological performance—in this religious framework, but these are usually frowned upon and never allowed to become normative elements within the structure or context of religious practice. A good example of such an aberration within religious practice in African Religion would be witchcraft.

Tanzanian Laurenti Magesa subtitled his book on African Religion "The Moral Traditions of Abundant Life."[29] He maintains that exploitation and manipulation do not count as virtues in this religious system. Similarly, Wole Soyinka in his fascinating book *Of Africa* has demonstrated convincingly how in the practice of divination in the religious tradition of the Yoruba the wellbeing of the devotee is paramount; indeed, the diviner or priest, known in the language as *Babalawo*, is unreservedly bound by the principle of gratuitousness. No reward is exacted and no toll is imposed for the practice of divination. Gratuity is reciprocated with gratitude.[30] This represents a practice that is diametrically opposed to and contradicted by the current ethos of material reward or economic dividend that characterizes the performance of healing, prophecy, and deliverance in certain expressions of Christianity in Africa.

I reserve the term "prophetic practice" for religious approaches or expressions that are not averse to probing the structural roots or causes of crisis, violence, and social dysfunction, but do so while drawing on the core values of their respective traditions to strengthen and enhance the wellbeing of adherents. Examples of such core values from the Christian tradition include justice, solidarity, compassion, mercy, charity, and ecological stewardship.

Also, an understanding of Jesus Christ is of vital importance in this mode of religious functioning. Prophetic practice takes into account the entire gamut of the gospel narratives, including sacrifice, self-denial, suffering, and commitment, dimensions that are patently absent from the Christological preferences of pathological performance. Further, an in-depth understanding of Jesus Christ must include the interplay of his human and divine attributes, which comprise the whole variety and gamut of human emotions in the gospel narratives.

Quite clearly the way that I use the term "prophetic practice" has an obvious resonance with "praxis," especially as this latter is construed and applied in the tradition of liberation theology. But there is a difference: prophetic practice is not contrasted with orthodoxy; the conceptual and practical opposite of prophetic practice is pathological performance.

The key point here is that just as there is a cast of pathological performers who are active in the African religious landscape, there are, similarly, prophetic practitioners. At an institutional level the tension between both orientations can be acute, but there is no doubt in my mind about their respective credentials. It would be misleading to identify either of the two approaches exclusively with particular denominations.

In chapter 3, I mentioned the religiously motivated strife that pits the mainly Muslim coalition Séléka against the predominantly Christian militia anti-balaka in the war-ravaged country of Central African Republic. In that context, Cardinal Dieudonné Nzapalainga, archbishop of Bangui, together with Rev. Nicolas Guerekoyame-Gbangou, president of the country's Evangelical Alliance, and Imam Oumar Kobine Layama, president of the Islamic Council, offer a striking model of prophetic practice. Often referred to as the "three saints of Bangui," these religious leaders are at the forefront of a countrywide initiative to promote peace, tolerance, and coexistence among Muslims and Christians. Since the violence began, the three have organized rotational prayer sessions in the Catholic cathedral, the great mosque, and the Protestant churches in Bangui. They concentrate on promoting "peace schools," where children of all religions can study, as well as establishing mixed healthcare centers open to everyone, irrespective of religious or ethnic background.

In light of this example, Gifford's assertion that "Catholicism, in contrast to Pentecostalism, is very reluctant to countenance any form of enchanted Christianity"[31] would seem problematic. The reason, he maintains, owes largely to "a process of NGO-ization" in which Catholicism becomes preoccupied with "development—historically schools and clinics, but now development in the widest possible sense, often human rights, justice, and peace."[32]

There can be no doubt about the central and effective role of Catholicism in promoting human and social development in Africa, especially in the provision of education and healthcare to millions of Africans through church-affiliated or church-sponsored institutions. Gifford goes as far as to argue that Catholicism "is the biggest single development agency on the continent,"[33] and multiple examples support this claim about the role of the Catholic Church in the promotion of integral development. Gifford describes one example:

[I]f one wanted to sum up in one word the role of Kenya's Catholic Church, it would be development. Blessed with enormous resources, educated personnel and extensive grassroots networks, the Catholic Church is a development agency without parallel. Development extends to every activity, although schools and hospitals are still the most obvious.[34]

Similarly, there are countless individuals within Christian communities across the continent whose secular occupations and religious initiatives contribute positively to the re-imagination and reconstruction of the socioeconomic, cultural, and political fabric of Africa. They do not seek to exploit or manipulate; rather their prophetic practice that seeks to counter dehumanizing socioeconomic and political forces is a concrete manifestation of their religious allegiance and affiliation.

Nonetheless, I disagree sharply with Gifford's position that "the more Catholicism has opted for development, the more it has ceased to cater for or appeal to Africans with an enchanted religious imagination. . . . Enchanted religious concerns, not addressed by official Catholicism, are catered for by Pentecostals."[35] When we examine closely the patterns of religious growth in contemporary Africa, we see that neither pathological performance nor prophetic practice is the exclusive preserve of any one denomination. From a Catholic perspective, the church in Africa is prone to both. Through an increasing phenomenon of the "pentecostalization" of Catholicism, modern-day clerics have preyed upon the gullibility of the wealthy and the vulnerability of the poor, much as others have contributed to the transformation of their social context and the creation of an enabling environment for the reduction of poverty and attainment of development.[36] Like their Pentecostal counterparts, several Catholic clerics have become specialists in the so-called ministries of healing, prophecy, and deliverance. The tactics are the same; so are the expected material rewards.

In this chapter I have attempted to critique the way religion, in particular Christianity, functions in Africa. In her book, *Replenishing the Earth: Spiritual Values for Healing Ourselves and the World,* the late Kenyan Nobel Peace laureate Wangari Maathai states: "I remain hopeful that, especially in sub-Saharan Africa, religion will become a liberatory experience."[37] Encouraging signs of prophetic practice should give cause for hope, yet pathological performance does not appear to be waning.

Current evidence supports the view that religion has a future in Africa. How that future develops or whether or not it is sustainable will depend to a larger, not lesser, extent on the interplay between prophetic practice and pathological performance. The latter purports to proffer simple solutions to the trials and tribulations of devotees and in many instances ensnares well-intentioned and desperate adherents in a cesspool of unfulfilled aspirations. Yet the false allure of its ideology often proves irresistible both for "society's losers" and the "Christian elite" in Africa.[38]

Conversely, prophetic practice strives to exemplify core religious values for a sustainable and meaningful flourishing of human existence. Given the appeal and sophistication of pathological performance today, especially in the age of digitalization and information technology, genuine prophetic practice will struggle to register an enduring impact for the vast majority of religious adherents and devotees on the continent. One particularly hopeful development is the growing consciousness and groundswell of resistance to religious pathological performance by disillusioned and disaffected adherents and devotees.

In Islam and in Christianity more and more examples are emerging in which Christians and Muslims have found common cause in denouncing, resisting, and overcoming virulent strains of religious performance that unleash a regime of terror on innocent Muslims and Christians. They are plumbing the depths of their religious traditions to reclaim the core values of mercy, tolerance, peace, justice, compassion, and graciousness in contrast to the agendas of peddlers of sectarianism.

In the case of Christianity, both pathological performance and prophetic practice draw on Christological sources, and proponents reference an infinite amount of scriptural texts to bolster their appeal. When Jesus of Nazareth posed the ultimate Christological question, "Who do you say I am?" little did he imagine that he was unleashing an avalanche of responses that would shock and awe followers two thousand years hence. The theological and scriptural resources of Christianity can be channeled toward Maathai's idea of liberatory prophetic practice *and* they can also be pressed to serve dehumanizing pathological performances. A test of a sound theology is the ability to spot the difference, while exposing the Christological bankruptcy of the latter.

Veteran African churchman Henry Okullu once observed poignantly: "Everywhere in Africa things are happening. Christians are talking, singing, preaching, writing, arguing, discussing. Can it be that this is an empty show?"[39] That is the question.

Notes

1. "The Kanungu Massacre: The Movement for the Restoration of the Ten Commandments of God Indicted" (The Uganda Human Rights Commission Periodical Report, 2002). Available at http://www.ais-info.org/doc/informes/2002%20The%20Uganda%20Massacre.pdf.

2. http://www.bbc.com/news/world-africa-32412212.

3. Brendan Carmody, *African Conversion* (Ndola, Zambia: Mission Press, 2001), 19.

4. Ibid.

5. Paul Gifford, *Christianity, Development and Modernity in Africa* (London: Hurst & Company, 2015), 13–28.

6. Birgit Meyer, *Translating the Devil: Religion and Modernity among the Ewe in Ghana* (Edinburgh: Edinburgh University Press, 1999), 175.

7. http://www.pewforum.org/files/2010/04/sub-saharan-africa-chapter-3.pdf.

8. See Philip Jenkins: *The Next Christendom: The Coming of Global Christianity* (Oxford: Oxford University Press, 2002), 85–89.

9. John L. Allen, Jr., *The Future Church: How Ten Trends Are Revolutionizing the Catholic Church* (New York: Doubleday, 2009), 23–26.

10. See Jenkins, *The Next Christendom*, 85–89, and Allen, *The Future Church*, 28–29.

11. "The Hopeless Continent," *The Economist*, May 13, 2000; "Africa Rising," *The Economist*, December 3, 2011; "A Hopeful Continent," *The Economist*, March 2, 2013.

12. Paul Gifford, *New Dimensions in African Christianity* (Nairobi: All Africa Conference of Churches, 1992); *African Christianity: Its Public Role* (Bloomington, Indiana University Press, 1998); *Christianity, Development, and Modernity in Africa* (London: Hurst & Company, 2015).

13. Emmanuel Katongole, *The Sacrifice of Africa: A Political Theology for Africa* (Grand Rapids, MI: Eerdmanns, 2011), 40.

14. Gifford, *African Christianity*, 348.

15. Benjamin C. Ray, *African Religions: Symbol, Ritual, and Community* (Upper Saddle River, NJ: Pearson, 2000), 45.

16. Ibid.

17. Magesa, *What Is Not Sacred? African Spirituality* (Maryknoll, NY: Obis Books, 2013), 69.

18. Gifford, *African Christianity*, 20.

19. Ibid., 27–28.

20. https://www.ghanaweb.com/GhanaHomePage/regional/Tony-Aidoo-jabs-Duncan-Williams-299751.

21. Paul Gifford, *Christianity, Politics and Public Life in Kenya* (New York: Columbia University Press, 2009), 86ff.; *Ghana's New Christianity: Pentecostalism in a Globalizing African Economy* (Bloomington and Indianapolis: Indiana University Press, 2004), 161–69.

22. Philip Jenkins, *The New Faces of Christianity: Believing the Bible in the Global South* (Oxford: Oxford University Press, 2006), 101.

23. https://www.ghanaweb.com/GhanaHomePage/regional/Tony-Aidoo-jabs-Duncan-Williams-299751.

24. Peter Oduor, "Power and Religion," Daily Nation, January 24, 2014.

25. R. Scott Appleby, "Religious Violence: The Strong, the Weak, and the Pathological," Practical Matter, no. 5 (Spring 2012): 1–25.

26. Karl Maier provides a vivid account of how the gospel of prosperity preys on the gullibility of African elites and the desperation of the African poor, especially women, in This House Has Fallen: Nigeria in Crisis (London: Penguin, 2000), 251–67.

27. Gifford, Christianity, Politics and Public Life in Kenya, 241.

28. R. Scott Appleby, The Ambivalence of the Sacred: Religion: Religion, Violence, and Reconciliation, Carnegie Commission on Preventing Deadly Conflict (Lanham, MD: Rowman & Littlefield, 1999).

29. Laurenti Magesa, African Religion: The Moral Traditions of Abundant Life (Maryknoll, NY: Orbis Books, 1997).

30. Wole Soyinka, Of Africa (New Haven, CT: Yale University Press, 2013), 148–50.

31. Gifford, Christianity, Development, and Modernity in Africa, 151.

32. Ibid.

33. Ibid.

34. Gifford, Christianity, Politics and Public Life in Kenya, 81.

35. Gifford, Christianity, Development, and Modernity in Africa, 151–52.

36. For a more comprehensive and positive appraisal of the contributions of faith-based organizations and churches in Africa to development, see Deryke Belshaw, Robert Calderisi, and Chris Sugden, eds., Faith in Development: Partnerships between the World Bank and the Churches of Africa (Oxford: Regnum, 2001).

37. Wangari Maathai, Replenishing the Earth: Spiritual Values for Healing Ourselves and the World (New York: Doubleday, 2010), 164.

38. Karl Maier, This House Has Fallen: Midnight in Nigeria (New York: Public Affairs, 2000), 264.

39. Henry Okullu, Church and Politics in East Africa (Nairobi: Uzima Press, 1974), 54; quoted in Tinyiko Sam Maluleke, "Half a Century of African Christian Theologies: Elements of the Emerging Agenda for the Twenty-First Century," Journal of Theology for Southern Africa 99 (1997): 8.

5

Healing the Earth, Healing Humanity

A chicken develops a headache when it sees another chicken inside the cooking pot.

—African proverb

So far my narrative has advanced and developed the argument that African Religion is the ground in which Christianity and Islam are planted. The roots of these religions reach deep into a foundational indigenous spirituality that prioritizes life, communion, and solidarity throughout Africa, and they find nourishment there. I have also contrasted African Religion's inherent proclivity to explain, predict, and control, with the tendency of some contemporary performances of Christianity to adapt this approach to manipulate, influence, and exploit the beliefs of adherents.

My principal aim now is to examine how the dynamics of African Religion explore the nexus of creation, salvation, and ecology, so important in our twenty-first-century world. I believe that African Religion offers useful insights to understand this nexus or connection. Although there is a dearth of published material in African theological research dealing with the significant question of ecology, awareness is growing that the blend of culture and spirituality practiced on the continent provides additional resources for spiritually grounding ecological stewardship and responsibility.

I recall a BBC World Service radio program that assembled a panel of religious leaders to examine the issue of climate change and religion in Africa. The panel, consisting of a Catholic archbishop, a Muslim leader, and a Pentecostal pastor, candidly admitted the tardiness of religions in Africa in general to appreciate the gravity and engage the problem of climate change. Yet this delayed engagement is not for lack of available resources in our African traditions.

Such resources include the personal witness of African leaders like Wangari Maathai whom I have already referenced. Her life and work remain a beacon of hope in the global quest for an ecological ethics of stewardship, respect, and care for the environment. Also, her writings reveal several aspects of the ecological credentials of African Religion, and its resources are directly complemented by insights from the thoughts of Emeritus Pope Benedict XVI and Pope Francis.

Part of the underlying rationale for my narrative, ideas, and examples derives from my conviction that ecology represents a new frontier for theological ethics in African Christianity, and that Christianity has much to learn from African Religion. I maintain that by reclaiming the "animist" dimension of this religion we are properly able to appreciate its contribution to the ecological debate and project. Animism, in the sense that I understand it, affirms the basic belief that all of reality is enfolded in a divine caress and animated by the life-giving breath of the Spirit. Trees, animals, and water are sacred elements, and human beings have the duty to care for and protect them. To destroy or pollute them incurs the wrath of the gods and goddesses with which they are associated and also the sanctions of the community.

The sad reality, though, is that as human beings we have so hurt the earth that it seems as if we are consciously daring or totally skeptical of talk of divine wrath. Although it is not in doubt that we face an existential ecological crisis, there is no shortage of doubters of the science and the reality of the crisis. A story from my early life will perhaps place this crisis in context.

Tears of a Woman

In Benin City, Nigeria, where I was born, a river flows eastward. The origin of the river called Ikpoba flows out of the mist of myth and folklore. Details are sparse but the people of Benin believe that the river was formed from the tears of a jilted lover of the same name. Disconsolate, heartbroken, and inconsolable, Ikpoba wept and wept and wept until her tears turned into a stream. Then in the rush of her tears she dissolved and the stream became a river. Because the people of Benin believe that Ikpoba flows from the tears of a woman who was unjustly treated, they venerate and revere the river.

Ikpoba was the object of awe and fascination for me as a child growing up in the city. The story had caught my imagination and I longed for any opportunity to be by the river. Also, Ikpoba was a source of life supplying fresh water in abundance to meet the assorted needs of the people. One of the earliest proverbs I heard as a child emphasized the importance of this and other water bodies: *Ẹzẹ i mwen eghian*, which literally translates as "a river has no enemy" or "water has no enemy." Besides being ubiquitous in proverbs, fresh water provided the inspiration for the naming of many of my relatives, as it did for many more people in Benin City. *Amẹzẹ* is a cousin, her full name being *Amẹzẹ i si ọfọ*, meaning "fresh water doesn't cause perspiration." *Amenaghawon* is another cousin, her full name being *Amenaghawon i lẹ s'omwan*, meaning "the water reserved for you will never run from you" or "a person's destiny is unique." My favorite, *Amenovbiyegbe*, metaphorically depicts water as a sibling in a Franciscanesque manner— "water, my mother's child." More strikingly, this practice of naming is reinforced by a communal spirituality that venerates water as a deity of abundance and prosperity, such as my mother's goddess, *Olokun*, who in her aqueous essence regulates the wellbeing of humans.

Ikpoba has three bridges, but the oldest, a smaller and narrower steel bridge, has since fallen out of use. A newer, bigger, and wider bridge made of concrete connects the city to the east and the north of the country. The third bridge is invisible but the people of Benin City believe that Ikpoba is a bridge between two worlds—the world of human beings and the world of their gods, goddesses, and ancestors. When devotees seek to encounter their deities they go to Ikpoba, where earth unites with sky and where tears of lamentation flow endlessly and copiously, like those of Rachel of the Hebrew Scripture (Jeremiah 31:15). To this day, Ikpoba is the site of rituals, worship, and religious sacrifice, especially rituals that have to do with compassion, forgiveness, and reconciliation.

The sadness of the story of Ikpoba comes from another source today. Although devotees continue to visit the river for religious purposes, the river is now a pitiable shadow of its former glory. I recall Ikpoba as a fast-flowing deep body of water, with strong currents and the busy traffic of boats ferrying fishermen and goods back and forth. Now it has been reduced to a narrow shallow stream that is silted and polluted. Worshipers still come by night, but during the day its banks hold the busiest carwash stations in town. Polluted with dirt, sewage, and effluents, its slow-flowing mud-brown waters perpetually froth with suds from assorted detergents pumped into the river by the carwashes.

If indeed a woman named Ikpoba once lived, the pain of her betrayal would hardly have rivaled the agony of today's pollution and desecration by the very people she exists to nourish and refresh with the waters of life. Her plight calls to mind the poignant words of Pope Francis: "Never have we so hurt and mistreated our common home as we have in the last two hundred years" (*Laudato Si'* 53). There is no injustice quite so appalling and alarming as that visited on mother earth by human beings.

The Enemy Is Us

Multiple signs and consequences demonstrate our ecological transgressions. They include the pollution of air, water, and soil; rising sea levels, melting snow caps, deforestation, desertification, loss of natural habitats and biodiversity, and increased competition for dwindling and limited resources. The intense debate around these issues emphasizes the imperative and urgency to "save the planet" and "heal the earth," a rhetoric that contains familiar religious resonances.

Despite the stridency of naysayers, I have little doubt that human beings are largely responsible for the hurt and mistreatment of the earth. Such is the gravity of this ecological abuse that, as Francis puts it, "The earth, our home, is beginning to look more and more like an immense pile of filth" (*LS* 21). Ikpoba is a painful reminder that the earth is crying out, and so are millions of its poor women and men with reduced access to fresh water and food sufficiency. Across Africa, several water bodies have suffered the same fate as Ikpoba: Nairobi River, River Niger, Lake Victoria, Lake Chad, and the list continues.

When the pope declares that we are hurting the earth, we do not have to take his word for it. Francis is not an environmental scientist, but he is right. A landmark study by the Lancet Commission on Pollution and Health has found that pollution of the air, water, soil, and in workplaces is the largest environmental cause of disease and death in the world today and is responsible for an estimated nine million premature deaths. The figure of one death per every six people far outstrips the tally of deaths from AIDS, malaria, and tuberculosis. The contamination of air and water is the leading cause of death. Unsurprising, the vast majority of pollution-related deaths occur in poorer countries, many of which are in Africa. In Chad and Madagascar, pollution accounts for a quarter of all deaths. At over 92 percent, Somalia tops the global all-time table of pollution-related deaths.[1]

The Lancet report also finds that, in addition to the burden of death, the economic cost, especially for already impoverished countries, runs in the trillions of dollars. The earth is groaning under the weight of pollution and can no longer carry its burden. This terrifying realization "threatens the continuing survival of human societies." There is no argument about who is to blame: *we* are the enemy. "Human activities, including industrialisation, urbanisation, and globalisation, are all drivers of pollution."[2] We are hurting the earth and hurting ourselves.

Pope Francis has also noted that "If we are truly concerned to develop an ecology capable of remedying the damage we have done, no branch of the sciences and no form of wisdom can be left out, and that includes religion and the language particular to it" (*LS* 63). Yes, the task of healing the earth goes beyond any single discipline; it must connect the domains of science, spirituality, and ethics. In addition, Wangari Maathai has advanced the idea that an ecological commitment is a "commitment to service" that manifests itself in "caring for the earth,"[3] which signals possibilities for healing the planet and humanity. Likewise, the wisdom of African religious traditions, long derided and dismissed as animistic, offers resources for cultivating sound ecological virtues to stimulate a renewed commitment to humanity's shared responsibility to care for our common home.

Creative Animism

Wisdom from traditional African Religion sets it apart from the dominant approaches in the Judeo-Christian traditions but also complements them. A first principle is that the earth, our mother, is the outcome of an intentional act by an agent who is deeply involved and invested in the process of creating the world and human beings. As I have already pointed out, African religious traditions allow for multiple creative agents with some playing the role of the intermediaries or secondary agents who actually complete the process of creation. This highlights the relationship between the so-called "secondary," "lesser," or "economic" gods and goddesses and the "Supreme Being."

Second, notwithstanding the impression we get from the Judeo-Christian narratives of creation, the claims to "dominion" or "subduing" the earth are neither absolute nor unilateral. Positively construed, such a claim implies a duty of care, usually rendered as a form of "stewardship." Although this may sound positive, in the Judeo-Christian tradition, nonetheless, stewardship seems a one-directional reality that flows from human beings toward other creatures. In other words, it assumes that other creatures or constituents of nature do not have any, equal, or reciprocal responsibility of stewardship toward human beings. Herein lies a critical difference: African Religion emphasizes the mutuality and interdependence that underline the communion and solidarity of human beings and the rest of creation. This is fundamental.

Third, this earth is the subject of an ongoing renewal in time and in space. Creation was not a definitive act sequestered in an impenetrable and irretrievable historical past. Creation is an enterprise continually being fulfilled, in mutuality and reciprocity. The focus is not so much on how the earth came into being as it is on how it is to be continued and sustained, how it survives. The plan can go awry, and human beings can mistreat the earth, as the story of Ikpoba and the Lancet Report concur. Conversely, human beings can chart a different course, one of care and protection of mother earth.

Fourth, the duty and responsibility of healing, replenishing, and renewing the earth is a communitarian experience. Essential to my argument is the conviction that healing the earth is primarily about healing humanity. How we treat mother earth is an accurate measure of how we treat ourselves. Any wound inflicted on nature is a wound inflicted on ourselves. This is a pivotal dimension of the present ecological crisis. Healing the earth sets us on a path toward the survival and salvation of humanity, toward healing ourselves.

I believe that the spiritual imagination embodied in African Religion can make a unique contribution to our joint planetary responsibility. At a time when "saving the planet" and "healing the earth" dominate the global discourse on sustainability, climate change, and ecological integrity, these four principles of African Religion can help cultivate appropriate and effective ecological virtues.

Ecological Gratitude

As noted early on, missionary Christianity and scholarly discourse of a particular ideological bent derided and still portrays African Religion as animist, with all the derogatory connotations this term implies. Judging by my experience as a practitioner of African Religion and my understanding of it from a theological perspective, in its truest sense animism represents a creative process of ecological wholeness and solidarity.

As an animist, I look upon trees and bushes and an assortment of vegetation as resources for "healing ourselves and the world," to borrow the subtitle of Wangari Maathai's book. The earliest and sometimes only form of medicine that was practiced in my family was herbal. It consisted of concoctions, solutions, roots, tree bark, leaves, ointments, salves, and various remedies derived from plants and animal by-products and organs. This was the case for most ailments not directly connected to malicious human or spiritual agency.

At the root of this attitude lies the belief that *the human person and the cosmos have a vital connection* and that both influence and depend on each other. In the words of Congolese theologian Bénézet Bujo, "one can only save oneself by saving the cosmos as well."[4] Maathai articulates a key component of these ecological virtues as gratitude and respect for the earth's resources—"the gratitude we ought to feel for *what the earth gives us.*"[5] These words help us begin to perceive the meaning of this belief in mutuality, reciprocity, and interdependence. Gratitude for what the earth gives us is akin to gratitude for what a mother gives a child; an African proverb says that a child can never (re)pay for its mother's milk.

My experience of African Religion tells me that its approach to environmental ecology is not solely theoretical. Its distinctive approach and tradition of spiritual awareness infuses all of creation and transforms it into a sacramental reality. As Bujo says, creation is experienced and reverenced as a revelation of God who triumphs over death to save both humankind and the cosmos.[6] The result is a moral imperative or duty to care for our common home.

In its true sense animism avoids any exploitation of nature. Instead, animism demonstrates that "care for the environment affects the quality of our relationships with God, with other human beings, and with creation itself. It touches our faith in and love for God."[7] In this understanding, life represents an expansive reality and a continuum. Life is not construed only as a reality constituted by the living; it also includes the ancestors and the yet-unborn—in other words, all the constituents of nature.

My animistic upbringing has resulted in what I call a holistic perception of the universe. Wellbeing is conceived of as harmony and integration among the four ecological siblings of self, others, the spirit world, and nature. Such wellbeing has a core principle that is formulated by Maathai as "love for the environment." This entails not only taking "positive actions for the earth," but is demonstrable as a lifestyle of solidarity expressed at times in lamentation or rage.

> If we love the environment, we must identify with the tree that is cut down, and the human and other communities that are dying because their land no longer

sustains them. We must express regret for the destroyed landscapes, become angry when we hear of another species under threat from human activity or see another polluted river or a landfill.[8]

Harmony and integration epitomize a healthy humanity and a healthy universe. South African anthropologist Harriet Ngubane sums up harmony and integration as follows: "For a Zulu [read African] conceives good health not only as consisting of a healthy body, but as a healthy situation of everything that concerns him [or her]. Good health means the harmonious working and coordination of his [or her] universe."[9]

In sum, from the perspective of African traditions of spirituality *ecology* means more than a physical environment of organisms and inanimate objects; at a much deeper level, ecology constitutes a universe of spiritual meaning and ethical imperatives. In chapter 1 I used the term "ethnosphere" to emphasize the importance of looking beyond the material, scientific, and technical realms to deeper sources of ethical warrants and spiritual rationale for environmental sustainability and ecological harmony. Essentially, therefore, from an animist's perspective, a person's sense of self is intimately tied with his or her relationship with this universe; concern for ecology, therefore, can never be viewed as a cold and detached matter. The earth exists as a gift that is to be received and nurtured with gratitude. When Pope Francis declared the care of our common home a work of mercy, such work implied "a grateful contemplation of God's world" that "allows us to discover in each thing a teaching which God wishes to hand on to us" (*LS* 85, 214).

It is not surprising, then, that in African religious traditions reverence and protection for the environment are not optional. Rather, healing the earth is a religious experience and a moral imperative. Restoring the harmony between humanity and nature is a mutually beneficial experience of wholeness.

The belief systems and religious practices in parts of Africa demonstrate why this reverence is so ingrained, why it percolates in the religious sensibilities of even the staunchest Christian or Muslim on the continent. How do we explain the resilience of a sense of a living and moral universe in the framework of African spirituality? First, as should be evident by now, the belief is strong that the natural universe is both the origin of life and the source that sustains it. Consider the following account by Maathai, writing about Mount Kenya:

> For the Kikuyus, Mount Kenya, known as Kirinyaga, or Place of Brightness, and the second-highest peak in Africa, was a sacred place. Everything good came from it: abundant rains, rivers, streams, clean drinking water. Whether they were praying, burying their dead, or performing sacrifices, Kikuyus faced Mount Kenya, and when they built their houses, they made sure the doors looked toward it. As long as the mountain stood, people believed that God was with them and that they would want for nothing. Clouds that regularly shrouded Mount Kenya were often followed by rain. As long as the rains fell, people had more than enough food for themselves, plentiful livestock, and peace.[10]

The sad reality is that Mathaai's nostalgic description, like the tears of Ikpoba reduced to a trickle over centuries, is also a narrative of the devastating effects of man's inhumanity to mother earth. The present-day reality of melting snow caps, drying rivers, and drought is far removed from the idyllic portrait of life at the foot of Mount Kenya.

A second factor in the resilience of an African ecological sensibility is the common understanding that nature provides the needed materials for repairing and restoring life at its most vulnerable moments of ailment or infirmity. Not only do human beings exercise a duty of stewardship toward creation,

creation reciprocates by virtue of "*what the earth gives us*" for remedying individual and collective malfunctions. The duty of ecological care is not one directional, whereby human beings take care of creation, nature, or the earth as mindless disinterested stewards. Instead, this duty consists of a mutual pact: creation, the earth, or nature in turn takes care of all forms of life. In *Theology Brewed in an African Pot,* I give the following example of nature providing material for repairing a vulnerable and ailing human person: "In *Things Fall Apart,* when Okonkwo's young daughter, Ekwefi, took ill in the middle of the night, he immediately 'took his machete and went into the bush to collect the leaves and grasses and barks of trees that went into making the medicine for *iba* (fever).'"[11] My parents would have done the same whenever a child came down with fever, malaria, constipation, or other illnesses.

Such anecdotes can be construed simply as manifestations of a "belief in spirits" that inhabit natural objects, in other words, magic or superstition. Then it is easy to dismiss such practices as arcane and passé, or animist. However, experts who work in the field of pharmacognosy and study medicines derived from natural sources such as plants have scientific proof of the potency of some plants as remedies for a variety of ailments.

For example, one of the most effective treatments for malaria, Africa's worst insect-borne enemy, is plant-based Artemisia and neem. In my multiple travels and journeys across the continent, I always arm myself with a pack of malaria medicine based on Artemisia. An article on malarial prevention noting the efficacy of neem to target larvae of a particular kind of malaria-bearing mosquito concludes: "Neem oil has good larvicidal properties for *An. gambiae s.s.* and suppresses successful adult emergence at very low concentrations. Considering the wide distribution and availability of this tree and its products along the East African coast, this may prove a readily available and cheap alternative to conventional larvicide."[12]

I remain convinced that this spirituality of mutuality and interdependence offers Christianity and the global community of faiths yet another tool to proclaim the virtues of stewardship, simple living, reverence, and a covenantal relationship with our environment. Such a mutuality can serve as a powerful antidote to what Francis identifies as "the unbridled exploitation of nature" (*LS 67*).

Ecology as Fullness of Life

The central purpose of the regular ablutions with water from the medicine room, described in chapter 1, was to fortify our bodies and spirits against harm and diseases. In simple terms, these ablutions were a form of defense and a protection of life. In the tradition of the faith of my father and the spirit of my mother, the foundations and purposes of our way of being as Africans can be summed up under the rubric of "life." As Bujo points out, cultural systems in Africa thrive on the idea that "the strengthening and the growth of life are the fundamental criteria" for determining the ethical quality of humanity either as individuals or as a people.[13] Similarly, in the words of Magesa,

> Everything is perceived with reference to this [life]. It is no wonder, then, that Africans quickly draw ethical conclusions about words and actions of human beings, or even of "natural" cosmological events, by asking questions such as: Does the particular happening promote life? If so, it is good, just, ethical, desirable, divine. Or, does it diminish life in any way? Then it is wrong, bad, unethical, unjust, detestable.[14]

Across the variegated landscape of Africa, the continent's spiritual and religious imagination pivots on the understanding that faith, belief, and practice are about saving or "preserving human life and its 'power' or 'force.'"[15]

To grasp the deep meaning of this principle of life, we need to think of life as more than just biological perpetuation. As I have already mentioned, for me, as an African—or as an animist—"life" represents the ultimate common good, the shared patrimony of the group, and the burden of mutual care that is incumbent on each member. Life has a social quality that translates into a sacred space, or an ecological commons. This social quality is inclusive of the claim to life and the fundamental rights of every member, especially the poor and the underprivileged.

"Life" encompasses the universe of plants, animals, and nature. Life is the guarantee of wholeness and universal harmony within and between the material and the spiritual realms. Furthermore, life implies an unconditional duty or responsibility to action. In other words, as human beings, we have a moral imperative toward what Maathai calls "self-betterment" or "the belief that one can improve one's life and circumstances—and the earth itself."[16] To be morally upright is to act deliberately in favor of human life in all its dimensions. The sum of this spiritual and religious worldview aligns perfectly with Francis's idea that "There can be no ecology without an adequate anthropology. When the human person is considered as simply one being among others, the product of chance or physical determinism, then 'our overall sense of responsibility wanes'" (*LS* 118). This relationship between nature and humanity is vital. What affects the former affects the latter. What we do to the earth we do to ourselves and to others. Saving one implies saving the other.

The fate of humanity and the fate of the earth are inscribed in the same ecological book. As I see it, African religious traditions blend well with the pivotal idea that Benedict calls the "book of nature," Saint Francis of Assisi calls the "magnificent book" (*LS* 12), and Pope Francis calls God's "precious book" (*LS* 85).

A somewhat disturbing fact is worth mentioning in connection with the principle of life as constitutive of the African religious worldview. We need to be careful about romanticizing Africa's predilection for life. A close look at the continent today reveals no shortage of instances where life in whatever form appears to be under siege, and it is happening beyond the banks of the Ikpoba. In Libya and Somalia, states have collapsed, leaving in their wake lawlessness, chaos, and violence that daily scar the lives of people. Widespread corruption causes political dysfunctionality, which also takes its toll on people's lives. Lack of access to quality maternal healthcare means that several countries in Africa still have an elevated maternal mortality ratio. Surely Africans who plan and execute terrorist attacks on innocent civilians do not champion the principle of the sanctity of human life. It is not possible to wish away or ignore these disturbing realities. While I hold firmly to the belief that life is the "foundation and purpose" of culture and spirituality in Africa, I am equally and painfully aware of cultural and societal malfunctions that undermine and threaten human and environmental ecology.

Life as the foundation and purpose of African spirituality forms part of a larger claim, that of the community or family. Community and relatedness are central to the way in which most Africans understand themselves as human beings in society.[17] In the African religious and cultural perspective, community defines the space where the human person is situated, where he or she strives through personal actions to realize his or her full potential in cooperation with other members of the community. Because life is construed as a shared value or the ultimate common good, that is, in the spirit of *Ubuntu*, African spirituality allows for a wide participation of all members in setting the criteria for determining the common good and for judging people's actions.

The focus on community has three dimensions. First, it prioritizes the human person as the privileged recipient and custodian of the gift of creation, and it underscores the centrality of the human person within the ecological framework. Second, community is the privileged space for manifesting the sacred, for celebrating in ritual and worship, where the living and the world of the spirits intertwine and interact for the common good of the members of the community. To deprive the community of this vital interaction is to bring about its potential destruction, because the spirit world and the natural environment are part of a vital ecological pact. Third, as already mentioned, life is inclusive of our ecological siblings and other constituents of nature, and, thus, the experience of healing in its fullness occurs within this wider communitarian framework.

African Religion considers the realm of the natural environment charged with and inhabited by a multiplicity of spirits, even though beliefs that underpin respect for environmental ecology are prejudicially construed as "animism" and "paganism." Such pejorative terms, however, ignore the critical element that Bujo describes as an "interdependence of forces" between human beings and the cosmos that allows each to influence and affect the other. Such is the intensity of this vital connection—in Francis's terms, "integral ecology" (*LS* 137)—that "one can only save oneself by saving the cosmos." The consequences of this ecological interdependence are weighty. For Francis, "The human environment and the natural environment deteriorate together; we cannot adequately combat environmental degradation unless we attend to causes related to human and social degradation" (*LS* 48). And Maathai offers a corrective to the misconception that human beings and the natural environment function as two polarities. As she puts it,

> Nature is not something set apart, with or against which we react. It's not a place we fear as something within which we might lose our humanity or, conversely, a place where we might gain perspective and simplicity away from the corruption and treachery of the court or the city. It is, instead, something within which human beings are enfolded.[18]

This understanding of ecology, both human and environmental, resonates with a uniquely African spirituality and approach to creation in which creation acquires a sacramental dimension as a text inscribed all over with the actions of a God who triumphs over death to save both humanity and the cosmos. Worship, praise, and celebration in Africa Religion are suffused with rites and rituals that draw upon nature as a source and an inspiration for liturgical action.[19]

This spirituality and ethical imperative of reverence for nature, whether human or environmental, contains a powerful reminder that the duty to protect and preserve "environmental ecology" and "human ecology" originates from their constitution "not only by matter but also by spirit" (*Caritas in Veritate* 48), something an animist would clearly understand and celebrate. In the final analysis, this understanding obviates any tendency to dismiss African Religion pejoratively as animist and pagan. This religion concurs with Christianity in recognizing creation as a gift, freely given for our responsible use, which entails a responsibility of compassionate care and faithful stewardship.

Ecology as Covenant

Various global efforts seek to redress multiple forms of devastation of the natural environment. Such efforts would gain effectiveness if they were predicated on, or at least be open to, a premise that is not exclusively technological. I agree with Francis and Benedict that religion matters and faith matters. I do not mean this primarily in the sense of organized affiliation and practice, but by what people believe about themselves and about their environment. Science and technology have important roles to play in understanding and formulating responses to the ecological crisis confronting humanity in this twenty-first century. Spirituality and ethics have equally important roles to play in this ecological enterprise of healing the earth. For "Our relationship with the environment can never be isolated from our relationship with others and with God. Otherwise, it would be nothing more than romantic individualism dressed up in ecological garb, locking us into a stifling immanence" (*LS* 119).

At the root of an indifference to ecological concerns is a certain distorted understanding of faith and belief that contributes to the loss of a sense of awe and respect for the environment. Maathai seems to agree with this emphasis on the faith dimension of ecological concerns:

> When European missionaries came to the central highlands at the end of the nineteenth century, they taught the local people that God did not dwell on Mount Kenya, but rather in heaven, a place above the clouds. . . . The missionaries were followed by traders and administrators who introduced new methods of exploiting our rich natural resources: logging, clear-cutting native forests, establishing plantations of imported trees, hunting wildlife, and undertaking expansive commercial agriculture. *Hallowed landscapes lost their sacredness and were exploited as local people became insensitive to the destruction, accepting it as a sign of progress.*[20]

What is at stake here is perhaps deeper than what technology alone can address or provide; it is more about recovering and appreciating the vital connection between human life and the universe that accommodates, surrounds, and supports it. This vital connection is critical for the survival of the universe, which includes the human race. Benedict makes this important point when he assesses the role of technology:

> It is necessary to completely revise our approach to nature. Nature is not simply a space that is useful or recreational. It is, rather, the place where man was born; his "home," so to speak. It is essential for us. A change

in mentality in this realm, even with the contradic-
tions it entails, must make it possible to quickly arrive
at a global lifestyle that respects the covenant between
humanity and nature, without which the human family risks disappearing. Hence, serious reflection must be
engaged in and precise and viable solutions must be
proposed.[21]

In their writings both Benedict and Francis use the word
"covenant"; this is a powerful, rich, and evocative term that
captures the vital connection between humanity and nature. It
is important to explore the various dimensions of the term and
how it clarifies the central points of this chapter:

- *Mutuality and solidarity.* "Covenant" presupposes
  mutuality and a shared interest between humanity
  and nature. Covenant is not an impersonal pact: it is
  deeply inter-personal and eminently relational. It means
  we are in a collective and personal relationship with
  nature and our environment. What affects us affects our
  environment and vice versa. I agree with South African
  theologian Peter Knox that "without taking a mystical
  approach, a first step toward the salvation of our planet
  must be developing a kindred feeling for the planet and
  every one of its inhabitants."[22] As in any covenantal
  bond, the mutuality is intensely affective and emotion-
  ally engaging. We are ecological siblings.
- *Durability.* Covenants are made to last; they are not
  changeable at the whim of the covenanters. More precisely, covenants include the lifespan of the mutual
  interests of the covenanters. If humanity is in covenant
  with nature, then it is permanent and *for life*—in the
  sense of "vital" and "in perpetuity."
- *Co-responsibility.* For a covenant to "work" both parties must also assume clearly defined responsibilities

and roles, as well as measurable and verifiable tasks. Covenant commits the parties to do something together, something that is not simply the responsibility of one party. In humanity's covenant with nature, the former honors, protects, and reverences the latter, while the latter sustains humanity in a variety of ways.

- *Communication.* Along with this idea of relationality is the notion of communication. We are in communication with nature and vice versa. This has nothing to do with a "tree-hugging" naturist fad. The essential point is that our environment is an extension of our deepest selves. Understanding ourselves is understanding our environment. Or as Maathai says, nature is "something within which human beings are enfolded." Nature, of course, does not speak, but it can manifest itself in ways that are indicative of the state of planetary health and the status of our covenant with the earth. Thus irregular and extreme weather patterns leading to drought and flooding; desertification as a consequence of deforestation; melting icecaps due to global warming, itself a consequence of greenhouse gas emissions—all these are a form of "nature-speak," calling humanity to take seriously the imperative of healing the earth and healing ourselves.

Throughout this chapter (and indeed this book) I have woven a personal narrative of religious consciousness, beliefs, and practices of African extraction to ground my exploration of African Religon and our ecological crisis. My intent in doing so is to demonstrate that, alongside a scientific and technological framework, the religious traditions of Africa offer the robust spirituality needed to cultivate the requisite ecological virtues and realize the objective of "saving the planet" and "healing the earth." From experience, I remain convinced of the capacity of the religious and spiritual traditions of Africa to proffer a means of renewal to humanity as a whole and assist in healing what Wangari Maathai calls "the deep ecological wounds visible across the world."[23]

These spiritual values of the African tradition of abundant life include respect, reverence, empathy, solidarity, mutuality, reciprocity, interdependence, generosity, gratitude, and compassion. Perhaps some examples will clarify these values.

Consider, for example, the parent who goes to the forest to collect herbs and barks for preparing a healing remedy for a sick child. Before wielding the machete, he expresses contrition for the damage to be caused and pleads with the plant or tree for an efficacious outcome. Or a hunter who apologizes to game he has just caught and explains why he needs it for food so he and his family will survive. What about a drum maker who presents a ritual offering to a tree and explains to it the purposes for felling it, that this isn't callous or mindless destruction because the drum to be made will produce joy for the people and praise for the gods and goddesses?

The most moving example of this ecological covenant is the practice in some cultures of planting a tree for every child that is born and a second tree where the child's placenta is buried. The child grows up with a sense of reverence and develops a deep and vital bond with his or her trees, nurtured by mother earth, similar to the relationship with his or her siblings. Such examples carry significant moral weight. To draw on Maathai's insights,

> [T]hese spiritual values, more than science and data, might be the basis for a true human partnership [with nature] among our leaders to achieve their ultimate objectives and avoid the cataclysms of melting polar ice, vanishing permafrost and glaciers, deforestation, erratic and failed rains, prolonged drought, drying-up rivers and lakes, parched landscapes, dying animals, and large populations faced with diseases associated with malnutrition.[24]

In my view, four points are important in order to expand our notion of the ethical imperative to heal the earth and heal ourselves in this age of ecological crisis:

- an affirmation of the *vital connection between human and environmental ecology*: the fate of one is linked to the fate of the other; like the chicken, we ought to develop a strong headache when we witness the ecological distress of our times;
- a restoration of *harmony or balance in creation*: "harmony" and "balance" provide an image of what healing and salvation look like in the age of global warming and climate change. We can think, for example, of the global climate compact to hold the increase in the global average temperature to well below 2 degrees Celsius above pre-industrial levels and to pursue efforts to limit the temperature increase to 1.5 degrees Celsius above post-industrial levels;
- a *holistic understanding of human and environmental ecology*: healing and salvation are inclusive experiences; nothing is left out or unredeemed;
- a permanent *covenant or communion between humanity and nature*: the task we are called to assume for the fate of the earth and our salvation is an ongoing relational and communitarian experience.

I firmly believe that these values of African spirituality offer a unique resource for the world in its quest for renewal and meaning that can animate and breathe life into ordinary, day-to-day living. They include an attitude of reverence toward human and natural ecologies, a spiritual sense of community, an understanding of life that is expansive and inclusive, a holistic understanding of creation, and a shared responsibility of stewardship for the wellbeing of the universe.

Finally, as I have already noted, I do not pretend to imply that African Religion and its attendant spirituality delineate an unspoiled terrain of harmony and peace. Mine is a modest claim, from the perspective of an animist, that a world that confronts the threat of climate change stands to gain from paying attention to the values, principles, and virtues cultivated in this spirituality, this *way of being* in the universe that is construed not as matter only but eminently as spirit. This way of seeing reality calls us to responsible ecological citizenship and it makes us ecological siblings with all of nature. Citizenship demands and imposes duties and responsibilities often assumed grudgingly in impersonal terms. The notion of ecological siblings makes it personal: it entails an abiding bond of interpersonal relationships, mutuality, and interdependence. We are never alone.

Notes

1. Pamela Das and Richard Horton, "Pollution, Health, and the Planet: Time for Decisive Action" (19 October 2017); available at http://www.thelancet.com/journals/lancet/article/PIIS0140-6736(17)32588-6/fulltext.

2. Ibid.

3. Wangari Maathai, *Replenishing the Earth: Spiritual Values for Healing Ourselves and the World* (New York: Doubleday, 2010), 164.

4. Bénézet Bujo, *The Ethical Dimension of Community: The African Model and the Dialogue between North and South* (Nairobi: Paulines, 1998), 10.

5. Maathai, *Replenishing the Earth,* 10; emphasis mine.

6. See Bujo, *The Ethical Dimension of Community,* 209–12.

7. The Society of Jesus, *General Congregation 35,* Decree 3, no. 32 (7 January–6 March, 2008).

8. Maathai, *Replenishing the Earth,* 101–2.

9. Harriet Ngubane, *Body and Mind in Zulu Medicine: An Ethnography of Health and Disease in Nyuswa-Zulu Thought and Practice* (London, Academic Press: 1977), 27–28.

10. Wangari Maathai, *Unbowed: One Woman's Story* (London: Heinemann, 2006), 5.

11. *Theology Brewed in an African Pot* (Maryknoll, NY: Orbis Books, 2008), 145.

12. Fredros O. Okumu, "Larvicidal effects of a neem (*Azadirachta indica*) oil formulation on the malaria vector *Anopheles gambiae*," in *Malaria Journal*, http://www.malariajournal.com/content/6/1/63.

13. Bujo, *The Ethical Dimension of Community*, 27.

14. Laurenti Magesa, *African Religion: The Moral Traditions of Abundant Life* (Maryknoll, NY: Orbis Books, 1997), 77.

15. Ibid.

16. Maathai, *Replenishing the Earth*, 135.

17. A. Okechukwu Ogbonnaya, *Communitarian Divinity: An African Interpretation of the Trinity* (New York: Paragon House, 1994), 14.

18. Maathai, *Replenishing the Earth*, 94.

19. Bujo, *The Ethical Dimension of Community*, 208–25.

20. Maathai, *Unbowed*, 5–6.

21. Pope Benedict XVI, "Technology Should Help Nature Develop along the Lines Envisioned by the Creator" (https://zenit.org/articles/green-pope-reiterates-call-for-human-ecology/).

22. Peter Knox, "*Laudato Si'*, Planetary Boundaries, and Africa: Saving the Planet," in *The Church We Want: African Catholics Look at Vatican III*, ed. Agbonkhianmeghe E. Orobator (Maryknoll, NY: Orbis Books, 2016), 237.

23. Maathai, *Replenishing the Earth*, 43.

24. Ibid, 172.

6

The Backbone of the Church or Gender Rhetoric

Women aren't the problem but the solution.

—*Nicholas D. Kristof*
and Sheryl WuDunn

A bird with one wing does not fly.

—*African proverb*

As is customary at the end of a synod, Africa's Roman Catholic bishops released a series of exhortations to mark the conclusion of the second African synod in 2009. Their exhortation to women began with the following words: "The Synod has a special word for you, Catholic women. You are often the backbone of the local Church. In many countries, the Catholic Women Organisations are a great force for the apostolate of the Church. . . " ("Message of the Synod," 25).[1] These inspiring words made it into *Africae Munus*, the final apostolic exhortation of Emeritus Pope Benedict XVI, but with one notable revision. Benedict's version reads: "In the local churches, you are a kind of 'backbone'. . ." (58).[2] The official version substituted "often" with "a kind of" and placed the word "backbone" in quotation marks. The changes piqued my curiosity.

As a non-native speaker of English, I was curious to explore the difference between "often" and "kind of" in this context. Was it a matter of stylistics or substantive change? According to reputable dictionaries of the English language, the adverb "often" denotes "many times, numerous occasions, repeatedly, frequently, in many instances," whereas the phrase "kind of" denotes "somewhat," "to some extent," and "often express[es] vagueness or [is] used as a meaningless filler." Besides, by placing the word "backbone" in inverted commas, the speaker implies that the word is dubious and, therefore, not to be trusted, which is striking in this context.

Some may choose to dismiss this as minor grammatical stylistics, but I see it in a different optic. In the interstices between "often" and "kind of" lies the abiding phenomenon of gender bias, imbued with multiple forms of covert and overt sexism. The differences between the two terms present new, contemporary, and pressing questions of the equality, the rights, and the dignity of women in the self-understanding of the community called church. This global phenomenon is widely replicated and deeply rooted in African cultures and communities.

Writing in *Evangelii Gaudium*, Pope Francis conceded the inevitability of confronting this phenomenon: "Demands that the legitimate rights of women be respected, based on the firm conviction that men and women are equal in dignity, present the Church with profound and challenging questions which cannot be lightly evaded" (104). This candid admission notwithstanding, time and again on questions of gender rights, equality, and dignity the church has appropriated negatively the query of Jesus of Nazareth in Cana, "Woman, what have I to do with thee?" (John 2:4; KJV) to buttress an exclusivist and reactionary ecclesiology.

As the little fox said to the little prince in Antoine de Saint-Exupery's classic of the same title, "Words are the source of misunderstandings." The purpose of this chapter is not to pick pointless quarrels with words, but to show how entrenched patriarchal and androcentric concepts not only neutralize the best-intentioned rhetoric but also mask the tools for marginalizing and excluding a category of people from the life and ministry of the church. I view this as a part of the ongoing exploration of the pathologies of Christianity in twenty-first-century Africa. And I intend to show how much Christianity has to learn from African Religion on the question of women's roles and responsibilities.

I admit that I am not really qualified to make this case. After all, as U.S. theologian James Keenan has candidly admitted, I am a permanent member of the clerical club, "a world of men, in which women are not present."[3] I am a beneficiary of ascribed privileges and entitlements offered by this "world of men." From where I stand, it would be dishonest to deny the existence of residual unconscious gender biases. That is why I am opting here to remain at the level of the spoken word and to attempt to assess its believability based on the reality of its application or the lack thereof. I do so as a person who sincerely believes that the glory of God is humanity fully alive and unhindered by discrimination or exclusion on account of gender. I begin by examining this question from the perspective of the theological self-understanding of church in Africa, and my conclusions apply largely to the situation of Christianity on the continent of Africa.

Numbers, Words, and Beyond

"Backbone" in anatomy refers to the series of vertebrae extending from the skull through the length of the spine that is responsible for keeping the human frame upright. Metaphorically, it signifies the chief support of a system or an organization without which the latter crumbles. Synonyms of "backbone" include mainstay, cornerstone, foundation, buttress, pillar, and tower of strength.

Documents of the first and second African synods apply these metaphors or their variants liberally to the role and participation of women in the church based on their large numbers. By now it should be clear to the reader how I feel about using numerical argumentation to demonstrate and substantiate the salience of any group within the Christian community, or the importance of the church in Africa within the world church. Yet the numerical superiority of women in the church in Africa is a fact; this is undeniable. What grates, however, is the rhetorical leap from statistical occurrence to normative pronouncement. It seems irrefutable to me that what women contribute or what place they occupy in the Christian community cannot be reduced merely to a demographic weight or a numerical denominator. Much weightier considerations hinge on the nature of faith, the dignity of the human person, and the inimitable quality of the gifts, talents, and competence of the people of God, irrespective of gender.

The first African synod of 1994 posed a pivotal question concerning the nature and identity of the mission of the church. The synod queried: "Church of Africa, what must you now become so that your message may be relevant and credible?" In posing this question, the synod set as its objective the task of generating a new model of the church that would be better suited to the context of Africa. In reply, the synod made "a fundamental option of the Church as family." According to the synod, the church in Africa understands itself as a family and therefore "family" should provide the framework of our understanding of the church. We think of the church and express its meaning in our lives as family. The second African synod in 2009 furthered this thinking by affirming that church as family exists to further the mission of reconciliation, justice, and peace.

Identifying the church as family is part of a wider claim regarding the centrality of the presence and participation of African women. This presupposes that a church that understands itself as family creates ample space for all members of the family to play various roles. But how can we declare the church a family without recognizing the pivotal role of women as ministers and leaders? The church called family is first and foremost *her family*. As theologian Tina Beattie has pointed out, "We cannot 'hear' the voice of God speaking to us through scripture and creation, unless we hear the voices of women made in God's image—including women who suffer and labor to give life, as the God of the Bible does."[4] Beattie continues: "It is not possible to arrive at a wise understanding of family life, capable of informing pastoral practice and doctrinal development, when women who in every culture are the primary caregivers and custodians of the family are excluded from the conversation."[5]

In many fields of ministry, women in Africa have an impressive pedigree as pioneers, leaders, and ministers. But if we remain at the level of rhetoric, we may be tempted to believe that all is well in the church in Africa, a church that declares with oratorical flourish that "in Africa the woman is at the heart of the family," or "The quality of our Church-as-Family also depends on the quality of our women-folk, be they married or members of the institutes of the consecrated life," or, as mentioned above, that she is "the backbone and the stability of the [church as] family." Although these affirmations seem undeniable, the reality is often quite different. Many African women who are essentialized and reified in these declarations are also exposed to various forms of discrimination within and outside the church.

What, then, do these declarations actually mean in terms of the models and practices of ministry, participation, and collaboration that the Spirit is calling forth within the church in Africa and the world? It is difficult to answer this question unequivocally. Yet the answer must at least imply that the quality of the Christian community and the credibility of its proclamation are seriously compromised if women are denied full and equal participation in the life of the church called family. Full and equal roles include, for example, responsibility for decision-making at all levels of *her* church, leadership in all domains of the church and society, and full participation in ministry.

What the two African synods of bishops seem to have realized is that there are consequences to claiming family as the defining mark of the church. The claim certainly challenges us to transform the prevailing images and practices of the Christian community in a way that embodies the positive values of family. One such value is hospitality, which is a mark of inclusiveness. It presupposes the unconditional welcome of all the members of the body of Christ. Or, as Francis would say, "The Church must be a place of mercy freely given, where everyone can feel welcomed, loved, forgiven and encouraged to live the good life of the Gospel" (*EG* 114).

Notwithstanding the pope's inspiring proclamation, there are indications that not all are truly welcome in the community called church. Despite the spirited attempt by Vatican II to entrench the priority of baptism as the fundamental criterion of ecclesial belonging and ministerial participation, the church in Africa still resembles the *societatis inaequalis* of Pius X (1835–1914), where lay people, in particular women, are still treated as second-class members of the church and inferior helpers of priests and bishops. The following is a recorded testimony of the superior of a women's congregation in West Africa:

[T]he attitude and behavior of ecclesiastical leaders toward women religious is often both oppressive and contemptuous. There are cases of the outright appropriation of the properties of the congregations of women religious. In their subordination to the clergy, the clergy dictate terms and expect unquestioning compliance. . . . Due to their quest for economic control, incompetent priests are appointed hospital secretaries, school administrators, and bursars in diocesan apostolic institutes run by and/or belonging to women religious. Priests are gradually abandoning the task of preaching the word to take over the ministries of women religious. . . . In addition, their lack of education for justice [has] made them [women religious] a source of cheap labor for the clergy and "glorified house keepers."

This testimony describes a reality that seems poles apart from the grandiloquent claim that the church is a family where all are welcomed on the basis of the equality and dignity of the human person. More importantly, it confirms how adeptly ecclesial leadership can pay lip service to the dignity and ministry of women in the church. Yet an inherently patriarchal interpretation of scripture and the influence of clericalism in theology ascribe subordinate and secondary roles to women, particularly in Africa. Anecdotal evidence suggests that to counter this trend some African women have joined or founded new religious movements, where they find outlets for their ministerial charisms by exercising liturgical leadership and ecclesial authority, especially in the ministry of healing. Some examples include Kenyan Bishop Margaret Wanjiru of Jesus Is Alive Ministries, Nigerian Archbishop Margaret Idahosa of Church of God Mission International, Apostle Eunice Gordon-Osagiede of Spirit and Life Bible Church, also from Nigeria, and Ghanaian Rev. Vivian Sena Agyin-Asare, co-founder of Perez Chapel International.

Evolution and Revolution

The criteria for assuming leadership roles in the Roman Catholic tradition and the reservation of ordination to male members remain sensitive subjects. Yet declaring these taboo seems a vestige of a dictatorial mode of governance that functions by laying down edicts, a style of governance that ultimately weakens the body of Christ and hinders the full realization of its evangelizing mission.

The second African synod (2009) made a sobering assessment of the status of African women in the African society, noting that "unfortunately, the evolution of ways of thinking in this area is much too slow" (*Africae Munus* 57). It continued:

> While it is undeniable that in certain African countries progress has been made towards the advancement of women and their education, it remains the case that, overall, women's dignity and rights as well as their essential contribution to the family and to society have not been fully acknowledged or appreciated. Thus women and girls are often afforded fewer opportunities than men and boys. There are still too many practices that debase and degrade women in the name of ancestral tradition. (*Africae Munus* 56)

The synod's assessment focused on what it calls "certain African countries." While the truth of this statement is undeniable, it belies the credibility and authenticity of the church's concern for the plight of women. By this comment I do not intend to impugn the validity of this concern. What I draw attention to—without undermining the church's active role in the empowerment of women in certain contexts—is the danger of rhetoric that focuses on "certain African countries" but deflects attention from the shortcomings and inadequacies within the church itself. As the English would say, "charity begins at home."

I agree with Emmanuel Katongole that "the major challenge facing the church is not simply pastoral, namely whether the church can recognize, affirm, and defend the dignity of women, but ecclesiological, namely whether the church can be the space and community where women feel particularly at home, and where their voices and gifts of leadership are welcomed and nurtured."[6] His line of thinking jibes well with that of Tina Beattie. Words don't create reality: deep conversion is needed to transform and change reality.

To be fair, the second African synod also admits of limitations and shortcomings that implicate the church: "Women in Africa make a great contribution to the family, society and the Church with their many talents and resources. However, not only are their dignity and contributions not fully recognized and appreciated, but [they] are often deprived of their rights."[7] In the face of this admission, the question that should concern us is why this is so.

The rhetorically embellished self-understanding of the church as family is replete with endearing terms, but it lacks any concrete realization, which poses a challenge and raises significant questions for the universal church. How inclusive is the church in understanding, defining, and assigning ministerial and leadership roles? Are the values of justice, equality, and fairness that the church holds up to secular society practiced in the community called church? Is the church willing to shed its attachment to doctrinal and theological norms designed to "keep women in their place"? The church of the global South is asking questions, and they are not just questions for the church in the global North.

Oftentimes we hear claims that these questions are not relevant for the church in Africa, because, Africa, as the argument goes, has more pressing issues. I contend that this line of thinking simply provides a fig leaf and exaggerates the so-called pristine exceptionality and innocence of the church in Africa. From my experience as an African theologian I know that other African theologians are asking these questions. Ivorian feminist Marguerite Akossi-Mvongo concludes her survey of public opinion on the ordination of women in the following terms:

> As a feminist who researches gender issues, I would love to say that women's access to all ministries or a church headed by women would be perfect, but this will not solve all the problems of the church. However,

the access of women to the priesthood would not fundamentally alter the faith and spiritual dimension of the church. The fundamental mission of spreading the message of Christ will probably be better done with women priests because in the current state, "the harvest is rich but the laborers are few" (Luke 10:2 NJB). I think the real obstacles are not spiritual but practical. The ordination of women would be a real upheaval and a challenge to the temporal structure of the church, but it would also be an opportunity to correct matters that do not reflect the face of Christ. [Consequently] the church we want would be more comfortable when it speaks of equal rights for all humanity.[8]

On the one hand, those who argue that ordination of women to the priesthood is far from being the most pressing issue in the church in Africa make a reasonable point. However, on the other hand, the credibility of arguments they use against it are far from proven. Access to health and education for Africa's poorest women and girls are critical issues, as is freedom to exercise their human rights and baptismal privileges in a conscientious and responsible way. These issues do not exist in isolation. As an African proverb says, "If one finger touches oil, it soon soils all the others." In other words, all these issues matter in the lives of women. For this reason, I consider rather unsettling the political parlance of prevarication practiced by some in Africa's hierarchy. Tina Beattie states the problem pointedly: "The bishops who represent Africa at the synod, for example, tend to gloss over the harsh circumstances of poor women's lives in their countries in order to present a united moral front against so-called Western decadence on issues such as women's reproductive rights."[9] To prioritize "a united moral front" over matters of human rights, dignity, equality, and justice seems to me a gross falsification of the gospel of life.

One critical area where, unquestionably, women have been the backbone of the church is in the Small Christian Communities (SCCs), especially in eastern Africa. The SCCs emerged in the 1970s as neighborhood associations or groups of Christians, under the auspices of the Association of Member Episcopal Conferences of Eastern Africa (AMECEA).[10] The option by AMECEA to develop SCCs as "local churches" pioneered a new ecclesiological reality in the region. Initially designed to evangelize and inculturate the church in Africa, SCCs have become alternative ecclesial communities that correct the anonymity and impersonality of large parish structures.

As Laurenti Magesa describes them, "SCCs were meant to be cells where the Christian faith would be intensely lived and shared. They were in fact seen as the ecclesiastical extension of the African extended family or clan."[11] Often represented in ecclesiological terms as "church in the neighborhood,"[12] they were to be small enough to facilitate close and meaningful relationships and flexible enough to respond to a variety of pertinent social issues in the everyday life of Christians. Joseph Healey describes SCCs as a new way of being church and "church on the move" under the inspiration of the Holy Spirit.[13]

Numerous empirical studies have observed the tendency of SCCs to attract a predominantly female membership, often leaving out influential male members of the community.[14] Writing about SCCs in Dar es Salaam, Tanzania, Christopher Cieslikiewicz notes that "one of the greatest challenges for the communities today is to succeed in getting men involved in the life of SCCs. . . . It has been noticed that SCCs tend to turn easily into simple prayer groups where the presence of women prevail."[15] Besides the gender imbalance, this phenomenon highlights a moral anomaly. Given the highly patriarchal cultures of Africa, particularly in eastern Africa, it is difficult, if not impossible, to create and sustain neighborhood Christian communities in which women assume leadership positions unhindered or where men are content to play subsidiary roles. It is not uncommon that the few men who participate in SCCs tend "naturally" to appropriate leadership positions in the communities; conversely, women tend to or are coerced to acquiesce to the authority of the male members of the Small Christian Communities.

Taken together, such practices consistently militate against the functionality and effectiveness of SCCs as a locus of ecclesial communion, pastoral cooperation, inclusive ministry, and equal participation. SCCs are not yet the revolution that many of its proponents make them out to be. Viewed from a wider perspective, the higher proportion of female membership of SCCs and their relative lack of effective authority mirror the priority given to male authority and control in the church as a whole. Such situations subvert an ecclesiological morphology predicated on a *rhetoric* of women as the backbone of the church. Notwithstanding, some theologians positively value the SCCs as a place where women "assume a voice in a patriarchal culture" as well as relative authority and prominence in the community of the church.[16]

Gender matters in the community called church, no matter how stridently custodians of patriarchy attempt to undermine its pertinence for the church in Africa. Few topics in Catholic theology have been so frequently distorted when viewed through the lenses of patriarchy and sexism. In Africa as elsewhere gender has never ceased being an integral aspect of faith and belief. On the basis of gender the role and participation of women and men are socially defined and doctrinally codified in church and society.

Despite these observations, the church in Africa has been a force for good in numerous situations and instances. Much of this has been demonstrated in preceding chapters. In addition, material evidence indicates that advances have been made in the public sphere on the matter of gender equality.

An Inventory of Inequality

According to a survey by the World Economic Forum, the *Global Gender Gap Report 2015*, the gap between men and women has narrowed in areas of economic participation and opportunity, access to basic and higher levels of education, political empowerment through representation in decision-making structures, and health and survival measured by life expectancy and sex ratio. What this report also shows is that progress is neither universal nor consistent. No country in the world has yet closed its overall gender gap. In other words, there is still no country on earth where women and men are fully equal. With the exceptions of Rwanda and Namibia, the majority of African countries south of the Sahara fall in the lower percentile in measures of gender equality.

Notwithstanding some positive indicators, such as those contained in the World Economic Forum survey, the catalogue of gender-based challenges that women face across the globe defies belief:

- the transcontinental trafficking of women for sexual and economic exploitation;
- sexual abuse as a criminal act and as a weapon of war;
- the use of women and girls as sex slaves in areas of violent conflict as, for example, in the ongoing conflict in South Sudan, or even perpetuated by U.N. peacekeepers in the Democratic Republic of Congo and Central African Republic;
- the exploitation of child labor, for example, in the cocoa farms in West Africa;
- the lack of equal educational opportunities, as, for example, in South Sudan, where fewer than 1 percent of school-age girls actually complete primary school;
- the persistent practice of female genital mutilation;
- the use of minors as suicide bombers by terrorist groups, as, for example, in northeastern Nigeria;

- the menace of early marriage, and the attendant problem of maternal mortality;
- domestic abuse;
- the targeting of homosexual women through the odious means of so-called "corrective rape";
- and the list goes on.

And we should not overlook the systemic links between gender and poverty, disease, and illiteracy, nor how various cadres of church officials have been complicit in the criminal abuse of minors and other vulnerable people.

This inventory is not intended to shock the reader's sensibility but to illustrate the enormity and gravity of issues that the Christian community cannot ignore if it practices what it preaches concerning "the women who make up more than half the church."[17] The Christian community continues to struggle against a perception in its history and theology that it represents an inherently patriarchal and clericalist institution. Strident as the verdict may sound, on the matter of gender equality and dignity the church in Africa still lags behind, as was pointed out by Benedict: "[U]nfortunately, the evolution of ways of thinking in this area is much too slow" (*Africae Munus* 57). Speed would be a relevant issue if there were an active process to achieve the propositions of the synod, like "the greater integration of women into Church structures and decision-making processes."[18] However, there is little credible evidence of any such accelerated intentional process. Here again, the rhetoric is heartening, but the reality is barely functional.

The continuing existence of structural, cultural, religious, and ideological barriers that impede the participation of women in all walks of life constitutes an injustice. Pointing fingers at social and political institutions outside our church does not help. The incontestable evidence of gender gap in the church is the centerpiece of my argument. As the Synod of Bishops on "Justice in the World" poignantly stated, "Anyone who ventures to speak to people about justice must first be just in their eyes" (40).[19] Like charity, justice begins at home. At the third session of the Second Vatican Council, during the debate about whether or not to admit women auditors to the council, Cardinal Leo Jozef Suenens, then archbishop of Malines-Brussels, Belgium, made an incisive remark: "Women," he stated, "I believe make up half of humanity." To my mind, any attempt to deny the gifts, talents, and contributions of half of humanity is morally objectionable, especially if this happens in the Christian community. It would amount to a form of injustice and a contradiction of the tenets of Christianity. The gospel is unequivocal in its affirmation of the equality and dignity of all human beings—that all are created equal in the image and likeness of God. This we believe and teach; and this, too, we must practice as church.

The Christian faith teaches the equality and dignity of all human beings, that all are created equal in the image and likeness of God. As I see it, the implications of this act of faith are momentous, both for church and for society. To put it simply, albeit starkly, as the body of Christ, either we believe that women are created by a just God or we are devotees of a lesser god. There are no other options.

Thus, as a locus of living faith through justice, gender must transcend mere rhetoric, of which there is no shortage in the official documentations and declamations of the church. It is reassuring, however, that Pope Francis has recently focused attention on the question of gender roles and participation in the church, reminding us of the danger of confusing and conflating "service" and "servitude." However we approach gender, it is never reducible to mere definitions or rhetoric. The images we have of the church shape the quality and tenor of the social relationships that we construct among members of the body of Christ. Modifications of this image using effusive and expansive rhetoric do not automatically alter reality or create just relationships. A challenge confronting Christianity in

Africa is the need to radically deconstruct the bases of inequality and then to reconstruct a more just arrangement—a task for which personal and institutional conversion is a fundamental prerequisite.

A community that consciously constrains and diminishes the space available to its members to contribute their talents and gifts ultimately asphyxiates itself. Besides, if that community refuses to correct the inequality and injustice that exist in its midst, such resistance can lead to more perverse outcomes, such as tension and division within the community. Such attitudes demonstrate another example of the pathological performance that I described in chapter 4. Such deprivations are self-inflicted and enable the custodians to maintain their positions even in the face of contrary evidence.

Untapped Leadership Potential

There are, as I have noted, African women who have founded and head churches in their own right as leaders and icons of independence and self-actualization. Considering the widespread absence of credible and competent leaders capable of driving development and transformation in Africa, I remain convinced of the potential of the untapped resources among the continent's women. The task of the Christian community is to recognize this obscured reality and invest resources to tap its full potential for the body of Christ. To repeat words of the second African synod, "Women in Africa make a great contribution to the family, society and the Church with their many talents and resources. However, not only are their dignity and contributions not fully recognized and appreciated, but [they] are often deprived of their rights."[20]

Regarding the contributions of women to the family, society, and the church in Africa, consider, for example, women like Burundian Marguerite Barankitse, who has dedicated her life to the task of bridging atavistic ethnic divides and reconciling mortal enemies long separated by mutual hatred, prejudice, and antagonism, with compassion and love;[21] CNN Heroes Award winner Sr. Rosemary Nyirumbe, of St. Monica's Tailoring School, Gulu, Uganda, and Angelina Atyam, also of Gulu, who are creating new opportunities for children brutalized and traumatized by rebel insurgency and government recklessness; and 2013 UN Nansen Refugee Award recipient, Sr. Angelique Namaika, in Democratic Rrepublic of Congo, whose personal and religious vocation is to rescue, rebuild, and restore the dignity of women victims of violence and war.

I could list many other examples, but in keeping with my principle about the potentially misleading use of numbers, I will stop here, although when Benedict spoke about African women as a "kind of 'backbone' of the church," he based his exhortation in part on their numerical strength ("because your numbers, your active presence and your organizations are a great support for the Church's apostolate"). If such elegant rhetoric is not translated into genuine action to invest in Africa's most underestimated and untapped resource—women—the moral credibility and theological integrity of the church in Africa are compromised. Women are the heroic foot soldiers who can bring about hope, transformation, and change.

In addition to this brief reference to these four remarkable African women, lest I too fall into the same trap of empty rhetoric, I offer a personal account of signs of change in the field of theological education, research, and scholarship.

African Women Changing the Face of Theology

From 2013 to 2016, I facilitated a three-year theological research project known as the Theological Colloquium on Church, Religion, and Society in Africa (TCCRSA). A primary objective of the colloquium was to develop, model, and sustain a new and innovative methodology for theological reflection, research, and study at the service of the church in Africa and the world church. For three consecutive years, the colloquium convened a community of African Catholic scholars doing theology or using Roman Catholic theological/ethical (re)-sources in their academic disciplines to identify, analyze, and study a wide variety of issues important to the church in Africa and the wider society.

The colloquium achieved some significant milestones, one of which was reflected in the composition and number of scholars who participated. Through its composition, method-ology, and focus, TCCRSA offers both a glimpse of the shape of theology in Africa today and the promise it holds for the world church. Nearly half the participants were women, both lay and religious, something new and different. A gathering of theologians where women are not the negligible and silent minority is unprecedented in Africa. At best it would have been composed of no more than a couple of African women theologians—a token representation.

Increasing accessibility to theological education by African women is a new and growing trend. Among the women par-ticipants, eight were completing doctoral programs in theology in six universities in Africa. Since then six have been awarded PhDs in theological ethics. The accessibility to theological edu-cation by African women is sustained by more funding avail-able to women for advanced theological studies. In addition, religious communities of women have realized the necessity of providing solid training and formation for their members out-side of the traditional domains of teaching, nursing, and cat-echetics. Similarly, the new generation of African women, some of them joining religious life, are much more motivated to venture into areas of studies such as theology and philosophy, typically reserved for ordained clergy. Across an ecclesial and theological landscape where they have been unrepresented, their voices ignored, and their contributions unacknowledged, a veil of invisibility and non-recognition is lifting, African women are taking a critical stand on substantial matters in church and society, speaking their own truths as scholars with passion, confidence, and authority. They are no longer content to be spoken about as passive objects in theological conferences, synodal exhortations, and patriarchal edicts by clerics and ecclesiastics.

It is not surprising that this new generation of theologically astute African women expresses their understanding of faith in a radically new way. These non-traditional positions open new paths toward action-oriented theological initiatives that can affect the religious, cultural, socioeconomic, and political contexts of Africa. It is still too early to imagine or predict the outcome of this unfolding story.

Another initiative in this narrative of progress of inclusive theological research and scholarship is the Circle of Concerned African Women Theologians, founded by the matriarch of African theology, Ghanaian Mercy Amba Oduyoye. The group's manifesto captures her idea of creating "for many women," "a safe place to reflect on and analyze these [pertinent] issues."[22] By adopting "circle thinking," a "circle approach," or a "circle method" of theological reflection, Oduyoye and her colleagues pioneered a new way of doing theology:

> The most important learning is that the motivation for African women's commitment to doing theology comes as a result of the inner conversion by concerned women theologians. It is not motivated by a need to confront; impress or even win the church or other religious institutions. If this were the case, we would give up because many do not read our works. Our goal is to make Theology in Africa fly by equipping it with the missing wing. A bird with one wing does not fly. African Theology without the story of the faith of the women of Africa is handicapped. The distinct gift that we bring to the Theology of Africa is to repair the imbalance.[23]

As Oduyoye further describes it, circle theology does not aspire to become a purely "intellectual exercise"; rather, the circle approach seeks to focus "on the issue at hand," that is, issues that matter.[24] One of those issues is the gap between what we declare about the centrality of women's presence in the church and the paucity of concrete actions that reflect this centrality.

Backbone of the Church

To return to the bone of contention. The African synod declared that women were often "a kind of 'backbone'" of the community called church, a fact so obvious it hardly requires justification. A simple thought experiment would allow us to ask this question: If we truly believe that women are the foundation, support, and cornerstone of the church, what would this church look like?

I put this question to a group of African theologians—women and men. In your vision, I asked them, what would a church in which women were the backbone look like? "Hmmm!!" replied one of them, initially. "Serious business, women in the Church; Mary Magdalene will like your essay!" I hesitate to read too much into this flippant comment, but it bears mentioning that derision, dismissal, and denial often lurk behind conversations that concern people "who make up half of humanity" and are the majority of the body of Christ. Here is a sample of the views and opinions of a group of African theologians to this question.

A church where the word "woman" refers first of all to co-workers or partners of God and not to a mass of servants of the clergy. Women who benefit from a solid formation which empowers them to stand confidently before God and side by side with their brothers. Feminism is not reducible to technical knowledge; rather, it is a paradigm based on [the] biblical audacity of the virgin, the spouse, and the mother. [A church where] We do not block our ears when women draw on their experiences to reflect on God and the church.

When the Synod said that women were the backbone of the Church in Africa, it was merely describing a fact: without women, the Church in Africa today would look like a family without a mother. And yet women cannot unleash their full potential because they are not given more space to participate in leading the life of the Church as Family. It means allowing women to take part in the process of decision making; to have equal opportunities in ecclesiastical education in order to grow in their understanding of the faith, and offer a more competent service to the community.

In a Church in which women are truly recognized as its backbone by virtue of their fidelity to the call to discipleship and proclamation of the Gospel, their commitment to passing on their faith to their children and in their parish communities, and their service to humanity through works of mercy and compassion towards the poor and marginalized, we deeply appreciate the variety of gifts given by the Spirit and the service to be done for the common good (1 Cor. 12). Too often patriarchy in society and Church, and clericalism, blur our vision and negatively influence our decisions and actions.

The church we want is the church for all where each and every one is [a] first-class citizen (Congar); where the subordination of one gender group (male-female, Greek culture) to another or one social group (slave-free, master-servant, Roman culture) to another is not the rule. Captured by the hymn proclaiming no slave/free, no man/woman (Gal 3:28), this church, the sphere of the Spirit, respectful of age (African culture), empowers all; it is the competent witness to the reign of God (Kingdom) in our troubled world; the "little flock" (Luke 12:32) witnesses to the society without discrimination as to social ranking/gender or race,[25] respectful of age, choice of way of life, etc. Could this church reinvent ministries such as widows, aged men and women, supervisors (*episcopoi*), etc.?

The backbone hosts the spinal cord, holds up the brain, protects the vital organs and enables movement and without which the human body would not survive. Therefore to say that women are the backbone of the Catholic Church must carry the same weight; without women the Church would not be able to exist. Therefore a church where women are truly the backbone is where the norm is women's presence, voice, experiences, gifts and wisdom not only in ecclesiastical structures as deacons, priests, bishops and Pope but in the active construction of theology and canon law. The entire formation of the laity from baptism to death would be imbued and shaped by women.

To give the final word to Beattie,

The single greatest transformation that needs to happen is the full and equal inclusion of women in the church's theological reflection and decision-making processes. Unless and until that happens, our understanding of what it means to be made in the image of God and to incarnate Christ's love in the world will continue to be distorted by an androcentric exclusivity that refuses to attend to the wisdom and the suffering of women.[26]

I have structured this chapter around the idea of women as the backbone of the church. My reflections recall my own religious experience in which women are truly the backbone. In chapter 1, I told the story of my mother's worship of her gods and goddesses, and I recounted my father's ritual practices.

What I did not mention is that my father was also a devotee of a god, *Awanuro*, whose chief minister was a woman. She conducted worship, led rituals, and officiated at the rites, although the majority of her community of worshipers were men. No one ever raised gender-based considerations to protest her principal role as leader and priestess.

For all the reproach directed at African cultural practices and the treatment of women, the spiritual traditions of the continent create equal space for women to practice in their own right. As my mother's educational background is rudimentary, she could not formulate or articulate concepts of doctrinal theology. Nonetheless, like so many African women who sought and found solace in their religious practice, she was her own priestess and unsubordinated to any male priestly class. Throughout Africa, like my mother, many African women function as vessels of the unfettered, creative, and active spirits of the gods and goddesses. African Religion, indeed, has something to teach the world church.

Notes

1. "Message" (http://www.vatican.va/roman_curia/synod/documents/rc_synod_doc_20091023_message-synod_en.htmland).

2. *Africae Munus* (http://w2.vatican.va/content/benedict-xvi/en/apost_exhortations/documents/hf_ben-xvi_exh_20111119_africae-munus.html).

3. James Keenan, "The Gallant: A Feminist Proposal," in *Feminist Catholic Theological Ethics: Conversations in the World Church*, ed. Linda Hogan and A. E. Orobator (Maryknoll, NY: Orbis Books, 2014), 225.

4. Tina Beattie, "Maternal Well-Being in Sub-Saharan Africa: From Silent Suffering to Human Flourishing," in *The Church We Want: African Catholics Look to Vatican III*, ed. Agbonkhianmeghe E. Orobator (Maryknoll, NY: Orbis Books, 2016), 176.

5. Ibid, 177.

6. Emmanuel Katongole, "The Church of the Future: Pressing Moral Issues from *Ecclesia in Africa*," in *The Church We Want*, ed. Agbonkhianmeghe E. Orobator (Maryknoll, NY: Orbis Books, 2016), 172.

7. African Synod, 2009: "Proposition, no. 47" (http://www.vatican.va/roman_curia/synod/documents/rc_synod_doc_20091023_elenco-prop-finali_en.html); *Africae Munus*, 55 (http://w2.vatican.va/content/benedict-xvi/en/apost_exhortations/documents/hf_ben-xvi_exh_20111119_africae-munus.html).

8. Marguerite Akossi-Mvongo, "The Church We Want: Ecclesia of Women in Africa," in *The Church We Want*, ed. Agbonkhianmeghe E. Orobator (Maryknoll, NY: Orbis Books, 2016), 250–51.

9. http://www.latimes.com/opinion/op-ed/la-oe-beattie-pope-francis-women-20150925-story.html.

10. Joseph Healey traces the origin of SCCs in Africa to the emergence of "Living Ecclesial Communities" in Zaire (now DR Congo) in 1961. See "Timeline in the History and Development of Small Christian Communities (SCCs) in Africa Especially Eastern Africa," http://www.smallchristiancommunities.org/africa/africa-continent/107-timeline-in-the-history-and-development-of-small-christian-communities-sccs-in-africa-especially-eastern-africa.html.

11. Laurenti Magesa, *Anatomy of Inculturation: Transforming the Church in Africa* (Maryknoll, NY: Orbis Books, 2004), 43; see also Christopher Cieslikiewicz, "Pastoral Involvement of Parish-Based SCCs in Dar es Salaam," in *Small Christian Communities Today: Capturing the New Moment*, ed. Joseph G. Healey and Jeanne Hinton (Maryknoll, NY: Orbis Books, 2005), 101.

12. Rodrigo Mejía, *The Church in the Neighborhood: Meetings for the Animation of Small Christian Communities* (Nairobi: St. Paul Publications-Africa, 1992); Alphonce Omolo, "Small Communities Light Up Neighborhoods in Kisumu," in *Small Christian Communities Today: Capturing the New Moment*, ed. Joseph G. Healey and Jeanne Hinton (Maryknoll, NY: Orbis Books, 2005), 110–14.

13. Joseph Healey and Jeanne Hinton, "Introduction: A Second Wind," in Healey and Hinton, *Small Christian Communities Today: Capturing the New Moment*, ed. Joseph G. Healey and Jeanne Hinton (Maryknoll, NY: Orbis Books, 2005), 4, 6.

14. See, for example, Elochukwu Uzukwu, *A Listening Church: Autonomy and Communion in African Churches* (Maryknoll, NY: Orbis Books, 1996), 118.

15. Cieslikiewicz, "Pastoral Involvement of Parish-Based SCCs in Dar es Salaam," 101–2. A similar challenge concerns the inclusion of

youth in Small Christian Communities or the formation of SCCs of the youth.

16. Anne Nasimiyu-Wasike, "The Role of Women in Small Christian Communities," in *The Local Church with a Human Face*, ed. Agatha Radoli (Eldoret, Kenya: AMECEA Gaba Publications, 1996), 181–202; Agatha Radoli, ed., *How Local Is the Local Church? Small Christian Communities and the Church in Eastern Africa* (Eldoret, Kenya: AMECEA Gaba Publications, 1993).

17. http://www.latimes.com/opinion/op-ed/la-oe-beattie-pope-francis-women-20150925-story.html.

18. African Synod, 2009: Proposition, no. 47 (http://www.vatican.va/roman_curia/synod/documents/rc_synod_doc_20091023_elenco-prop-finali_en.html).

19. https://www.cctwincities.org/wp-content/uploads/2015/10/Justicia-in-Mundo.pdf.

20. African Synod, Proposition no. 47.

21. Emmanuel Katongole, *The Sacrifice of Africa: A Political Theology for Africa* (Grand Rapids, MI: Eerdmanns, 2011), 148–92.

22. http://www.thecirclecawt.com/profile.html.

23. Ibid.

24. Mercy Amba Oduyoye, "Re-reading the Bible from Where We Have Been Placed: African Women's Voices on Some Biblical Texts," *Journal of African Christian Thought* 10, no 2 (December 2007): 6.

25. Carolyn Osiek and David L. Balch, eds., *Families in the New Testament World: Households and House Churches* (Louisville, KY: Westminster: John Knox, 1997).

26. Beattie, "Maternal Well-Being in Sub-Saharan Africa," 177.

7

The Flourishing of Religions

What a child sees from the top of a palm tree an elder can see laid on a bamboo bed.

—African proverb

In Madagascar on Sunday, September 27, 2017. I was invited to attend a Eucharistic celebration in one of the economically deprived and socially marginalized neighborhoods of Antananarivo, the capital city. To prepare me for this experience my host explained that the church was located in the *"quartier populaire"* with worshipers drawn mostly from the informal settlement of Anosibe or "big island." It would be one of five parish Masses, the first starting as early as 5:30 in the morning. "There will be many people," he added. What he omitted to tell me was the demographics of the congregants.

We arrived bright and early and we immediately faced a problem: we ran into a thick traffic jam of people. Practically every square inch of space was occupied by a sea of teenagers and children. It took an adept church marshal to open a path through the throng for our car to access the main section of the church compound. The Mass was a festive and animated affair. From start to finish groups of young people and children in a variety of colorful attires took turns performing one liturgical act after another, complementing the lead of the main presider. It was impossible to tell the choir apart from the rest of the congregation. Everybody sang, mostly a cappella. As the Mass neared its end three hours later, another youthful crowd was already milling around the church eagerly awaiting their turn to worship. "If you come back in the evening for the fifth Mass, you will see the same thing," said my host as we slowly and careful navigated our way out through the multitude of worshipers.

The Center for Applied Research in the Apostolate (CARA) at Georgetown University has observed that the 258 percent growth of the Catholic population in Africa since 1980 is due largely to increasing fertility rates, ruling out migration and evangelization as strong factors of growth.[1] This growth rate can be extrapolated to account for religious growth in general on the continent. But it is remarkable that this growing population is a worshiping and deeply religious population; even more remarkable is the youthfulness of the demography.

From the twin perspectives of statistics and demography Christianity in Africa is anything but a dying religion, and the same can be said of Islam. The Pew Foundation further argues that both religions have grown significantly at the expense of African Religion. However, I dispute these findings and believe that such conclusions reveal a fundamental ignorance of how religion works in Africa. The two religions are growing but not at the expense of African Religion. On the contrary their growth is predicated on their essential relationship with African Religion. The latter is the ground in which they are planted. Without this vital relationship neither Christianity nor Islam would be recognizable as *African* religions.

Where then lies the future of Christianity in Africa? As I exit the platform of storytelling, I make no pretense of gazing into a crystal ball but instead will draw upon my analysis so far. Should we expect Christianity to continue to thrive in Africa? I choose to respond in the affirmative because of reasons embedded in its evolutionary traits.

There is a key distinction between thriving as a religious community and thriving as a statistical phenomenon. Existing statistical studies suggest that the future is bright for Christianity in Africa. Africa is one of two regions (the other being Asia) in the world that are registering the largest growth of Christianity. As the CARA study of Catholicism suggests, much of that is due to high fertility rates and improving life expectancies:

> Fertility rates in Africa have remained higher than anywhere else in the world. Growth in the Catholic population accounts for 23 percent of all population growth in Africa since 1980. The percentage of the African population that is Catholic has increased from 12.5 percent in 1980 to 18.6 percent in 2012. Although the number of parishes in Africa increased by 113 percent—adding 8,055 worship sites—the ratio of Catholics per parish has gone from 8,193 in 1980 to 13,050 in 2012. Since 1980, the number of priests has grown faster than parishes (131 percent compared to 112 percent) but not as quickly as the Catholic population (238 percent).[2]

Based on these figures,

> By 2040, the population of Africa is expected to be 1.9 billion and fertility rates will remain above three children per woman over her lifetime, on average. Life expectancies will likely rise to 68 on the continent by 2040. . . . The 21st century will continue to be an era of significant population growth on the continent. If current trends in affiliation and differential fertility among religious groups continue, in 2040, 24 percent of Africans will be Catholic. This would result in a Catholic population of 460,350,000 in Africa.[3]

For leaders of Christian communities these phenomenal numbers are truly heartening. Akin to a CEO looking at the financial forecast for his or her organization, not a few church leaders would be justified in adopting the attitude of the wealthy property owner in Luke 12:19: "The future is bright, man! Relax, eat, drink, and be merry!" Besides, the studies suggest that neither migration nor evangelization will shape the future growth of Christianity. Growth will happen anyway, as long as Africans continue to reproduce abundantly.

Yet a close observation shows that church leaders—its pastors, evangelists, preachers, and prophets—are not resting on their evangelical laurels. Historically, religious fervor and activity have never been more intense than they are in the twenty-first century. We have never witnessed such religious effervescence across the continent, not even in the days of the pioneering African firebrands and stalwarts of the movement of independent Christianity, such as Isaiah Shembe (1870–1935), John Chilembwe (1871–1915), Simon Kibangu (1887–1951), and Samuel Oshoffa (1909–1985). I recall the poignant observation of Henry Okullu cited in chapter 4 that "everywhere in Africa things are happening. Christians are talking, singing, preaching, writing, arguing, discussing." Indeed, these are exhilarating times for religious growth on the continent.

Things Are Happening Everywhere in Africa

Religion is growing in Africa at an unprecedented pace. However, I still maintain that we miss an important factor if we assume that the flourishing of religions, in this case Christianity, rests solely on these impressive statistics. In addition to numbers and figures, other factors should be considered when explaining the burgeoning practice of religion.

One of the factors, that of conversion, is not new. Africa is a continent of the converted, as my narrative clearly demonstrates. I am not convinced that scholars have sufficiently considered the implications of the fact that Africans consider themselves as converted. Although the term "cradle" is sometimes used by Christians to self-identify with a denomination (cradle-Catholic or cradle-Anglican, for example), the reality is that many ordinary African Christians do not consider Christianity an inherent part of their religious heritage in the same way that, say, a European does. A residual religious sensibility or consciousness native to Africa situates an African Christian in a locus or confluence of religious experiences. In other words, while an African convert considers himself or herself a Christian and adheres to the teachings and demands of Christianity, he or she is not totally untouched by the influences of other religious traditions, such as African Religion. In particular instances such influences could result in or manifest as a combination of religious practices.

The typical Christian imagination in Africa—if ever there was such a thing—tends to be shaped by a religious extroversion, viewing Christianity as a religion of foreign provenance. Despite the existence of venerable historical traditions of Christianity such as the Ethiopian Orthodox Church, Christianity in Africa has retained an aura of foreignness. To embrace Christianity is to practice a foreign religion that came to us from "overseas." That foreignness is a factor of Christianity's European provenance.

Consider, for example, how some African languages name items of foreign (primarily European) origin for which there is no local name. The item is identified with a familiar and local equivalent but complemented with an adjectival possessive. Thus sugar is "white man's salt"; pineapple is "white man's palm nuts"; chinaware is "white man's plate." Transposed to the case of religion, Christianity is "white man's religion," at least so it often seems in the imagination of Africans. There is nothing ideological about this linguistic and psychological naming of the identity and meaning of Christianity. It is purely a matter of perception. Although some African scholars make colonial and post-colonial influences a *cause célèbre* of research and scholarship, the average African Christian does not wage an ideological battle with Christianity as a foreign religion. In fact, its foreignness can be a source of attraction and a strong impetus for conversion, as Robin Horton has pointed out. In an analogous manner, African preachers and pastors, Pentecostal and Evangelical, often claim status and fame for their connections and partnerships with overseas counterparts and churches. At religious events, such as crusades, conventions, and leaders' workshops, to have an expatriate guest preacher headline the event is considered a sign of a church's status and a strong attraction for crowds of participants.[4]

If Christianity is a "white man's religion" in a linguistic sense, how does this nomenclature translate? What is its equivalent in the African religious imagination? As I have argued consistently, there is such a thing as African Religion, even though missionary Christianity considered it too animistic or heathenistic to consider "doing business with it." The same attitude persists today in evangelical and Pentecostal Christianity. Too often these two branches of Christianity facilely and readily equate African Religion with demonic, satanic, and occult practices. But in spite of this sustained vilification and frontal attack on African Religion, the "white man's religion" has not succeeded in dislodging it from the religious consciousness of African Christians.

One well-known example of its persistence that I have resisted introducing into this narrative is the practice of Voodoo. I have hesitated because one cannot claim to adequately and justly explore the complexity and vastness of this religious worldview in such a brief narrative like this. In addition Voodoo has long been misunderstood by those who associate it with sinister and malevolent practices. Noneheless, Voodoo has acquired a much more openly political profile, and Benin Republic has declared an official national public holiday (January 10) to mark the Voodoo religion.

However it is understood, preachers, pastors, and evangelists may goad their followers to fear and loathe African Religion. Still others will clandestinely have recourse to it in moments of crisis. Whether driven by fear or circumstances, somewhere in the religious consciousness of Africans lies a counterpart to the "white man's religion." This counterpart functions neither as foil nor foe, much less a competitor or rival. It is simply the ground on which the "white man's religion" was planted and on which it continues to grow. As one African proverb says, a person who eats the fruit of a tree also eats the leaves, branches, trunk, and roots of the tree. So it is with Africans who have eaten the coveted fruit of the tree of Christianity; they continue to partake of its leaves, trunk, and especially, its roots.

In his novel *Things Fall Apart,* Chinua Achebe narrates an event where the first missionaries asked the elders of the land for a piece of land to build a church. In their wise and resourceful creativity, the elders convened to deliberate, following which they reached a consensus: they would offer the white men as much land as they wanted, but only in the evil forest, where spirits of the undead and unburied lurked menacingly. It was an offer that no right-thinking person would accept. As the story goes, to the amazement of the elders, the missionaries rejoiced greatly at the generosity of their African hosts. They promptly built their church, launched an evangelical drive, and began to reap the rewards of their missionary labors with increasing numbers of converts. "We have now built a church," announced the head missionary enthusiastically to the village community.

What the story goes on to reveal is that even though Christianity took hold and flourished in the village, judging by the number of converts, in the religious imagination of the converts, the church was built on and surrounded by the evil forest. Although they were conscious of embracing a new faith, they could not divest themselves of a worldview shaped and sustained by their beliefs in the gods and goddesses and spirits and deities of their land who had their abode in the evil forest.

No doubt the Christian edifice represented a novelty for the converts. Yet, constructed on the terrain of their religious worldview and imagination, it retained a certain familiarity. Any attempt to distinguish and separate the two beliefs would have been both academic and futile. In the imagination of converts, the local spiritual forces were present and active in the midst of the nascent Christian community, but the white man boasted a more potent fetish to contain their menace: "It was said that he wore glasses on his eyes so that he could see and talk to evil spirits."[5]

Christians Are Talking, Singing, Preaching, Writing, Arguing, Discussing

Africans have always been a converted people. To put it differently, the weight of history or the passing of time has not yet occluded the memory of our conversion to a Western religion. In making this claim I disagree with the late Ghanaian theologian Kwame Bediako who argued that Christianity in Africa be considered a non-Western religion; he saw it as the southward shift of Christianity's center of gravity to the two-thirds regions of the world. Demographics and statistics are easy data to mine to support such an argument, although any conclusions drawn may very well be misleading.

Religious conversion tends to generate passion, zeal, and conviction; converts have often been caricatured as "outsiders who weep louder and longer than the bereaved." In the West (or North), while Christianity seems to have succumbed to the deadening weight of cynicism, apathy, and secularist assault, new recruits in the South continue to fan the embers of a global religion that promises relief and prosperity in immeasurable measure. Yes, today in Africa Christians are talking, singing, preaching, writing, arguing, discussing.

A second factor to consider in the flourishing of Christianity in Africa is the nature of Christian evangelization on the continent. As noted before, Christianity in modern Africa began and took root largely as a religion of the poor. In sub-Saharan Africa, it continues to appeal strongly to the teeming masses of Africa's poor—indeed, enough to satisfy the wishes and predilection of Pope Francis for "a Church which is poor and for the poor." If this correlation of poverty and Christianity in Africa holds true, should we not expect a decline in religious affiliation and observance as Africans progressively climb out of the mire of poverty and economic inequality? The correlation between "economic development and a more equal distribution of income" and the decline in the number of churchgoers and religious affiliation is a widely assumed axiom in social science studies, and with the exception of the United States, many prosperous countries in the northern hemisphere confirm this trend.

Judging by the outcomes of the Millennium Development Goals or MDGs (2000–2015) of the United Nations there has been a significant reduction in the absolute number of people living in poverty in the world. Although still lagging behind, poverty reduction in Africa is a fact. Counterintuitively, however, I believe that economic development and rising income levels in Africa will trigger neither a decline in religious observance nor an increase in secularization. It seems that the inner dynamics of Christianity in Africa yield a double guarantee of prosperity.

On one level, Christianity promises economic prosperity and upward social mobility on the strength of the devotees' manifestation and generous sowing of faith. This approach, commonly identified as the "prosperity gospel," is popular and widespread to the point that some older historical churches have adopted forms of it in their liturgical and para-liturgical forms of worship. On a second and perhaps more important level, what is abundantly reaped as the fruit of faith must be vigorously protected. The enemy always lurks—dark, sinister, and satanic forces; century-old ancestral curses; and so much else for which African Religion is falsely accused and vilified. Thus sowing, reaping, and protection become the specialty of

Christian churches, particularly among denominations specializing in a prosperity gospel. The triple operating matrix of this gospel (explanation, prediction, and control), as I have demonstrated, is extracted from African Religion.

In other words, Christianity is often *aspirational* within the Christian denominations that win new recruits more successfully. Its benefits and rewards are set against a horizon of material abundance and socioeconomic wellbeing so that even if few achieve those benefits and rewards, the power and appeal of their testimonies are compelling enough to hold the masses of followers spellbound. The followers are captives to the idea of similar access to these tantalizing crumbs.

Understood and practiced as an aspirational religion, Christianity has a panoply of mechanisms to stir and sustain the aspirations of old and new converts. In the age of the digital media revolution there is no dearth of channels, avenues, and platforms for displaying the success of Christians who have made it. There is no reason to curtail the aspiration of others to gain such material success; prosperity is an evident blessing by God for those who are generous in sowing the seeds of faith.

Prophet T. B. Joshua describes himself as a young man raised by God from "a poverty-stricken home to lead an international ministry" and to become "a mentor to presidents," "friend to the widows and less privileged," and "a role model to his generation." What is left unsaid is that, like several of his peers who led megachurches, he sits at the head of a commercially prosperous religious organization that counts its earnings in multiple digits. While it is safe to note that not many African Christians aspire to the role of presidential mentors, as a continent of the poor the vast majority do aspire to the kind of prosperity that has become the hallmark of these prosperity-gospel churches. They sustain their hope on the evidence of those who have achieved prosperity, and those who have gained prosperity rely on their religious guides and mentors to safeguard and protect their just rewards and divine blessings.

Karl Maier has examined these double dynamics in terms of the greed and gullibility of the wealthy, on the one hand, and, on the other, the desperation of the poor. Both are lucrative terrains for merchants of a prosperity gospel.[6]

I realize that there is a certain lack of logic in my approach, which suggests that what is good for Africa's poor is good for Christianity. As long as Africa is impoverished, Christianity will always have a solid base. To the outsider, the way African Christians are talking, singing, preaching, writing, arguing, and discussing bears no evidence that Africa is the poorest continent on the globe. More importantly, and quite paradoxically, I believe that should Africa miraculously overcome endemic poverty and rise rapidly to economic prosperity, Christianity can expect to have an even more solid base. This may seem to challenge if not upend the prevailing canons of the study of religions. In fact, it is a tribute to the innovative resourcefulness of today's dealers of Christian evangelism in Africa. For richer or for poorer, Africans and Christianity are yoked for life.

The Root of All Evil?

There is a third factor that guarantees the flourishing of religions in Africa, and that is the nature and means of evangelization and missionary implantation. As we have seen, missionary Christianity coined many unflattering names for African Religion, chief among them "animism" and "heathenism." I have argued consistently that what missionaries termed animism was a caricature based on stereotypes and on the evangelical ignorance and hubris of people who considered themselves ambassadors of a civilized religion and way of life. To this day, various forms of Christian denominations still consider African Religion as demonic, satanic, and occult. To speak of an "ancestral" malediction or curse is an explicit reference to the nefarious effects of what is wrongly construed or harshly misjudged as African Religion.

One of the greatest missteps of missionary Christianity was to present itself as a substitute for African Religion. The challenge, however, was that the propagators of Christianity assumed that the nature of African Religion was the same as its own. In other words it was one religion or the other. Thus, in colonial times, with the backing of the superior might of colonial powers, and in this day and age with a sophisticated array of evangelical props, Christianity was assured victory over animism and heathenism. What the missionaries failed to understand is that a way of life or spirituality is different from an organized religion of creeds, doctrines, and dogmas. The latter are easily substituted and replaced, but not the former.

Rather than replace the African way of life, Christianity built over it; thus, as I maintain, Christianity is rooted in the soil of African Religion. This approach unwittingly drove African Religion deeper into the hearts of its converts. Like a tropical tree the leaves and branches of Christianity flourished, but the roots remained deeply anchored in the African way of life. These roots nourished and shaped the growth of Christianity over centuries of evangelization in Africa. When we reap the abundant fruits of missionary Christianity today, it is sweetened by the taste of these roots. This has a bitter taste for evangelical puritans, so they continue to attempt to wash away or dilute the roots with the waters of baptism and the awesome force of the so-called "Holy Ghost fire."

This missionary approach of substitution remains strong today but so do its roots. For Christianity to actually replace African Religion would amount to cutting off its own roots, which would result in a weakening of Christianity in Africa. This situation resembles a catch-22 scenario. Christianity will continue to flourish, but will also continue to be influenced by the manner and form of its relationship with African Religion.

Religion of the People, by the People, and for the People

The future of Christianity in Africa, for me, seems not unlike the wave of democratic uprisings that occasionally wash over Africa's socioeconomic and political institutions. We have seen instances of this phenomenon in the 1990s in sub-Saharan Africa (in places like Congo, Benin, Gabon, Mali, Zambia, and Zaire [now DRC]) and the early 2000s in North Africa (during the Arab Spring in countries like Tunisia, Libya, and Egypt). The outcomes may not have been long lasting, but each wave did have an impact and leave an imprint. Africa is always changing.

Africans do take their religion seriously. Religion works for them and so occupies an important place in their self-understanding, construction of meaning, and existential worldview. It is a means for making sense of existence itself and not just a cloak worn to protect against the vicissitudes of human existence. Believers, therefore, want to have a say in how it works. The religious elites of clerics and ecclesiastics may hold sway over doctrines and creeds, but the people invent freely and creatively their terms and modes of engagement in religion. In Africa to be spiritual is to contain a plurality of identities. The ability of many Africans to mix and match religious practices within a larger framework may seem to professional scholars as manifestations of syncretism or a form of religious schizophrenia. Adherents view matters differently: it is a form of translation that requires creativity and innovativeness, and a firm commitment to diversity.

For example, although women may be denied participation in decision-making and ministerial roles in some denominations, many find ways of practicing not only their faith but also of shaping the evolution of their beliefs. While clericalism may be on the rise in some denominations, other forms of ministry continue to thrive, propelled by the participation of a non-clericalized majority of Christians, that is, lay women and men, catechists and missionaries, volunteers and pastoral workers. According to CARA there are now an estimated 393,580 catechists in Africa, along with 7,195 lay missionaries, and 928 lay men and women in secular institutes. For these women and men, Christianity is as much their religion as it is that of the clerics.[7]

The concerns that Africans bring to their religion for answers and resolution are myriad; they include ethical, political, social, economic, cultural, and personal matters. Consider, for example, issues of reproductive health and human sexuality. Any minister who is attuned to the pulse of religious growth on the continent knows that many women are taking responsibility for their own reproductive health, and women and men are seeking new ways of living out their marital commitments. Human sexuality is no longer taboo, notwithstanding the collusion of religious institutions and political institutions to criminalize forms of sexual orientations deemed unnatural or ungodly.

In our highly globalized and digitized world, more Africans are emboldened to recognize, embrace, and celebrate their sexuality, even when patently hostile quasi-religious, cultural, and political institutions create an environment of fear, intimidation, and violence. Africans come in a stunning diversity of orientations, preoccupations, and expectations, but they all expect that religion will work for them—be it Christianity, Islam, or African Religion.

Statisticians predict future trends based on aggregating numbers, and the growth of Christianity in Africa has provided fertile ground for such studies, computations, and predictions. While statistics are often suitable for prediction, they are not very useful and even misleading in explaining or controlling religious phenomena in Africa. It is not sufficient to string up numbers and design demographic charts. Religion is much more important than such dry indicators of growth. For those who remain convinced of the importance of religion in their lives, there is great significance in its singular ability to enable them to explain and control their circumstances. Religion is about making sense of life and finding meaning in existence, even if the outcome isn't always favorable. Millions of slum dwellers flock to churches and mosques for solace and solutions, and while help may continue to elude them, they remain undaunted in their religious beliefs and practices. They continue to flock to religious spaces and events. Clearly, something bigger and stronger than numbers urges them on.

Identifying what lies at the heart of their convictions requires that we consider not only the exterior manifestations of faith and belief, but their underlying roots as well. Both dimensions are of critical importance. If the manifestations of the Christian and Islamic faiths continue to be strong in Africa, it is primarily because they are rooted in the fertile soil of African Religion. This is an inconvenient truth for those who have come to believe—on the basis of strong numerical growth—that Christianity and Islam successfully replaced and rendered otiose African Religion.

To what degree religion continues to work for Africans will be measured by how we honor a genuine quest for meaning, truth, and mystery sustained by our plural religious identities. As an animist and in my ongoing faith journey as a Christian, I feel fortunate to have known, lived, and experienced the benefits of the wisdom and insight of all these identities in my religious upbringing.

Notes

1. Center for Applied Research in the Apostolate (CARA) at Georgetown University, *Global Catholicism: Trends & Forecasts* (June 4, 2015), 25-26.

2. Ibid.

3. Ibid.

4. Paul Gifford, "Prosperity: A New Foreign Element in African Christianity" *Religion* (October 1990): 373-88.

5. Chinua Achebe, *Things Fall Apart* (New York: Doubleday, 1994), 149.

6. Karl Maier, *This House Has Fallen: Midnight in Nigeria* (New York: Public Affairs, 2000), 252.

7. CARA, *Global Catholicism*, 27.

CONCLUSION

Could This Be an Empty Show?

Several birds can fly in the sky without their
wings touching.

—*African proverb*

There was a time when I was not a Christian. . . . Although
my conversion to Catholic Christianity did mark a significant
milestone in my journey of faith, that journey began much
earlier. Long before the waters of baptism trickled down my
head on Holy Saturday, April 2, 1983, in St. Joseph Catholic
Church, Benin City, Nigeria, I had doused myself countless
times with the bubbly waters of the faith of my father and the
spirit of my mother preserved in the medicine room. Before the
chrism oil of confirmation was smeared on my forehead, my
arms had been incised multiple times and sealed with fortifying
potions prescribed by local diviners and herbalists. And long
before I partook of the Eucharistic meal, I had been nourished
body and soul by ritual meals offered in sacrifice to ancestral
deities. There was, indeed, a time when I was not a Christian.

Catholicism teaches that a sacrament is in the nature of
a seal, leaving an indelible mark. A sacrament can never be
undone. African Religion is rich in sacramental symbolisms
and metaphors, and water, blood, and food play significant

roles in its symbolic universe. Ablution and asperges for physical fortification, ritual cleansing, and ceremonial blessing are common visible practices of invisible transformations in the lives of devotees of African Religion. The same is true for blood drawn and mixed with herbal concoctions, and food offered in ritual worship. I was privileged to have experienced all these dimensions of its sacramentality. The implication is that I, too, like so many African Christians, have been sealed by the waters of the way of life of my ancestors. As I have argued throughout this book, it was pretentious for missionary Christianity to believe it could remove the seal of African Religion from the hearts of converts to Christianity in one fell evangelical swoop.

My claim that I have not always been a Christian may seem unsettling to some readers, but it is my way of celebrating my schooling in the truth and holiness of the way of life of my ancestors before encountering Jesus the Christ, now my way, my truth, and my life. Also, it is my way of recognizing and honoring the Spirit of God alive and active in the hearts of all women and men. That Spirit did not begin to stir in their hearts with the coming of Christianity or Islam, nor did the advent of these religions terminate the actions and deeds of the Spirit. In an unexplainably profound manner the Spirit bridges the pre-existent reality and the subsequent one, what existed before and what came afterward. Present reality is a composite of both. I am an African Christian, or to paraphrase the famous "I am an African" speech of former South African President Thabo Mbeki, today it feels good to be an African Christian.

I doubt that any African can claim to be solely and entirely Christian. To be a Christian in Africa is to accept a hyphenated and multipolar identity; it is to contain a plurality of identities. The universe of meaning, or what I have described as a spiritual *ethnosphere*, is constituted of intersecting paths of knowledge and wisdom, imagination and consciousness. It is the nature of the fertile religious soil of the continent in which any seed can grow. Christianity and Islam are seeds sown on this soil. Over the centuries they have taken root and flourished, undoubtedly along with some tares. Various academic disciplines interested in the growth of religion in Africa count the fruits of these long-sown seeds in millions of converts, adherents, and worshipers. As the seeds grow into trees, fruit is produced from those roots that reach deep down into the soil. That soil is African Religion.

An existential symbiosis thus exists between Christianity and African Religion, and between African Religion and Islam. The result of this symbiosis is the nature of the religious acumen of the African people. Although routinely excoriated by colonial missionaries and modern-day evangelists, they have a singular capacity to discover gems of truth in their ancestral way of life and to find new treasures in their received religious traditions. Recall that Jesus of Nazareth commended this capacity for religious creativity and innovativeness: "Therefore every scribe who has been trained for the kingdom of heaven is like the head of a household who brings out of his or her treasure what is new and what is old" (Matt 13:52).

There is an unmistakable relativity (I avoid the term "relativism") about faith and belief in Africa. The Igbos of eastern Nigeria say: "*Egbe belu, Ugo belu. Nke si ibe ya ebena, nku tije ya.*" This literally translates as: Let the kite perch and let the eagle perch too. If one says no to the other, may its wing break. In other words, "Live and let live." I have used several images to describe the vital relationship between African Religion and the two world religions of Christianity and Islam: a soil or ground on which the latter are planted, the foundation that holds up their edifice, and the roots that anchor and nourish a reality. The imagery of birds flying in the sky is equally apt. All religions on the continent, whether indigenous or imported, can lay claim to a patch of the African consciousness and imagination without entering into conflict with one another.

Although Christianity and Islam maintain a strong penchant for making absolute claims on truth and salvation, and in the process engender quarrels and hostilities, African Religion makes no such claims. Rather, it exhibits an inclusive hospitality and abhors proselytization. An African proverb says that "we can all see the sun from our own houses." Similarly, no single culture has a monopoly on the gospel. No single culture can exhaust the mystery of salvation. No religion has a monopoly on the truth. If one thing stands, another can stand beside it. The sky *is* wide enough for several birds to fly without their wings colliding.

It is worth repeating that no one culture has a monopoly on the gospel and no single culture can exhaust the mystery of salvation. From an African perspective the gospel of Christ is incarnated in culture; it is not a strange bedfellow of culture. The face of culture is capable of donning the face of the gospel and adorning it with the particular gifts of a particular people in a particular context, while remaining open to its transformative power. The gifts that each culture employs to proclaim the Christian message create a multifaceted tapestry of harmony, which is the opposite of bureaucratic uniformity or monotonous monoculturalism. Any imposition or importation of a culture dressed as the Christian message is antithetical to the transcultural value of the Good News. To insist on a monocultural rendition of the message of Jesus is alien to the evangelical commission to make disciples of all nations. All cultures that have been touched by Christianity and many more that will be touched by it should feel liberated rather than constrained.

In his encyclical *Evangelii Gaudium*, Pope Francis challenges evangelical monoculturalism and criticizes any mimicry or preservation of outmoded models of Christianity. As an African Christian, I rejoice in the fall of the old demons of cultural imperialism that were content to foist foreign pantomimes disguised as Christian truths on places and peoples with rich cultural capacities for receiving, translating, and incarnating the Good News of the risen Christ according to their own genius and in their mother tongue. The mystery of redemption in Christ reaches further and deeper than any single culture can claim to contain or exhaust.

In the twenty-first century Christianity and Islam have found a permanent home in Africa. The impressive numbers are more than sufficient evidence of their phenomenal growth over the last two centuries. I reiterate that this growth does not happen in isolation and that both religions continue to grow in symbiotic relationship with African Religion, their host. Those who have embraced either of these two religions have done so with a commitment and enthusiasm comparable to that of the first Christians. I have noted Henry Okullu's rhetorical question before: Can this be an empty show? Twenty-first-century Christianity in Africa is not an empty show any more than it was for faithful converts like Isidore Bakanja (1887–1909), Daudi Okelo (1902–1918), Jildo Irwa (1906–1918), Anuarité Nengepeta (1939–1964), Benedict Daswa (1946–1990), Charles Lwanga and scores of Ugandan martyrs in the nineteenth century who converted to the religion that they subsequently helped shape by their ultimate sacrifice.[1]

The sacrifice of these martyrs has borne tremendous fruit. Several studies show that there is no denying the fact that Africa is one of the places where Christianity is making the greatest gains. When we speak of the southward demographic shift of Christianity, Africa represents a significant and strategic evangelical locus where the future of Christianity shines the brightest. This fact, perhaps, explains why Emeritus Pope Benedict XVI spoke glowingly of Africa as "an immense spiritual 'lung' for a humanity that appears to be in a crisis of faith and hope." Yet, speaking of Africa as a place of spiritual regeneration and growth should not obscure the fact that it is also a place of appalling violence, suffering, and misery. It is a continent that knows the harsh reality and wears the agonizing face of poverty, violence, and suffering on a grand scale. For good and for ill, religion has played a part in this reality.

There seem to be two Christian churches on the continent. First, there is the church of the privileged: "a Church which is unhealthy . . . confined and . . . clinging to its own security. . . . [C]oncerned with being at the centre and then ends by being caught up in a web of obsessions and procedures" (*EG* 49). These are the leaders of the myriad denominations and hierarchies of Christianity and purveyors of the gospel of prosperity who enjoy the trappings of power, authority, and privilege. They do so at the expense of the impoverished masses of Christians who seek and hope for release from the clutches of poverty, violence, and misery, but constantly are fed platitudes and placebos laced with sanitized evangelical dictums. Such pseudo-evangelical and fundamentalist strategies are "a means of exploiting the weaknesses of people living in poverty and on the fringes of society, people who make ends meet amid great human suffering and are looking for immediate solutions to their needs" (*EG* 63). This approach to religion is a form of dangerous pathology.

The second church is that of the poor—men and women who epitomize faith as a living reality, who, like the Marcan widow (Mk 12:41–44), support the church even with the meager resources at their disposal. When Francis speaks of the "poor church" in *Evangelii Gaudium*, many are the manifestations of this reality among millions of believing Africans. This, in fact, is "a Church which is bruised, hurting and dirty because it has been out on the streets . . . ," a church where "so many of our brothers and sisters are living without the strength, light and consolation born of friendship with Jesus Christ, without a community of faith to support them, without meaning and a goal in life" (*EG* 49).

Although we can point accusing fingers at powerful forces and phenomena such as globalization, the commodification of human beings, the deification of a market economy, fiscal idolatry, and so on, the fact remains that "the church for the poor" ought not to be content to lament the maledictions and afflictions generated by these forces. Rather, Francis challenges this church to labor tirelessly to address the structural causes of poverty and make an ethical commitment to care for its victims. This represents a clear and present task of evangelization in Africa where masses of people are constantly convulsed and afflicted by poverty, violence, and suffering. It represents the imperative of a prophetic practice of the gospel message.

Missionary Christianity represents in large measure the origin of today's Christianity in Africa. Ironically, after a heroic mission to convert the "dark continent" Christian Europe droops under the excruciating weight of individualism, relativism, and secularism, which have almost succeeded in relegating the faith to the realm of irrelevance. The end result is pessimism and defeatism, compounded by what Francis calls "spiritual desertification" (*EG* 85–86). But can the churches of the North reach out to so-called young churches to find a means of spiritual resuscitation? This is where Africa and the rest of the global South can enter the stage as new evangelizers of the churches of the North.

There are many ways in which religion as practiced in the global South can become an evangelizing influence for global Christianity. One oft-forgotten gift of Africa to the world is that the good news is about "a joy ever new, a joy which is shared" (*EG* 2) and where all are called and welcomed to the feast (*EG* 4). When it comes to matters of faith, Africans exude joy in praise and worship, despite their challenges of poverty, violence, and suffering. Nonetheless, the joy of the gospel is constantly undermined by Africa's elusive quest for peace. The need for peace, a critical dimension of evangelization, represents yet another challenge and task for the church in Africa. Although the second African Synod (2009) recognized the significance of reconciliation, justice, and peace as constitutive dimensions of the evangelizing mission of the church in

Africa, not much has been achieved. The church in Africa must continue to work for peace and dialogue across the length and breadth of the vast religious, cultural, socioeconomic, and political landscape of the continent.

Africans do take their religion seriously. Whatever can be said about the tendency toward superficial and spiritualizing tendencies, for them religion matters. Religion works for them practically and beneficially, albeit, in some instances, pathologically. Some of the theology may be suspect and the zeal extreme, but not their level of conviction. This is not an empty show.

Africa's indigenous religious past has long been defined by negative categories, and its present is unfolding in a context of contestations, claims, and conflicts amid incontrovertible signs of vibrant growth. Its future, however, will rest on the spiritual resourcefulness of its people. By the middle of the twenty-first century the projected population of Africa will hit 2.5 billion and the share of the world's Christians living in sub-Saharan Africa is expected to grow from 24 percent in 2010 to 38 percent.[2] More Africans than ever before will have embraced Christianity as their primary expression of faith. Whether dominated by Christianity or Islam, Africa's religious heritage will thrive, flourish, and prosper in a soil animated and enriched by the faith of our fathers and the spirit of our mothers. Only in symbiotic relationship will all three religions prosper, for, as one African proverb says, a single bracelet does not jingle.

Notes

1. To read about Ugandan martyrs see J. F. Faupel, *African Holocaust: The Story of the Uganda Martyrs*, rev. ed. (Nairobi: Paulines Publications Africa, 2007); and James Martin, SJ, "The Story of the Ugandan Martyrs" (https://www.americamagazine.org/content/all-things/story-ugandan-martyrs).

2. http://www.pewforum.org/2015/04/02/christians/.

Suggested Readings

African Religious and Spiritual Traditions in Contemporary Scholarship

Laurenti Magesa, *African Religion: The Moral Traditions of Abundant Life* (Maryknoll, New York: Orbis Books, 1997).

Laurenti Magesa, *What Is Not Sacred? African Spirituality* (Maryknoll, New York: Orbis Books, 2013).

Festo Mkenda, SJ, Michael Amaladoss, SJ, Gerard J Hughes, SJ, Laurenti Magesa, and Diane B. Stinton, *The Way, the Truth, and the Life: A Confluence of Asia, Europe, and Africa in Jesus of Nazareth* (Nairobi: Jesuit Historical Institute in Africa, 2017).

Jacob K. Olupona, *African Religions: A Very Short Introduction* (Oxford: Oxford University Press, 2014).

African Christianity and Mission in History

John Baur, *2000 Years of Christianity in Africa: An African History 62–1992* (Nairobi: Paulines Publications Africa, 1994).

Kwame Bediako, *Christianity in Africa: The Renewal of Non-Western Religion* (Edinburgh: Edinburgh University Press; Maryknoll, New York: Orbis Books, 1995).

Adrian Hastings, *The Church in Africa, 1450–1950* (Oxford: Oxford University Press, 1996).

Adrian Hastings, *A History of African Christianity 1950–1975* (Cambridge: Cambridge University Press, 1979).

Elizabeth Isichei, *A History of Christianity in Africa: From Antiquity to the Present* (Grand Rapids, Michigan: Eerdmans, 1995).

Lamin Sanneh, *Disciples of All Nations: Pillars of World Christianity* (Oxford: Oxford University Press, 2008).

African Women in Theological Discourse

Teresia Hinga, *African, Christian, Feminist: The Enduring Search for What Matters* (Maryknoll, New York: Orbis Books, 2017).

Linda Hogan and A. E. Orobator, eds., *Feminist Catholic Theological Ethics: Conversations in the World Church* (Maryknoll, New York: Orbis Books, 2014).

Mercy Amba Oduyoye, *Daughters of Anowa: African Women and Patriarchy* (Maryknoll, New York: Orbis Books, 1995).

Wilfred Sumani, *Mothers of Faith: Motherhood in the Christian Tradition* (Maryknoll, New York: Orbis Books, 2017).

African Theology, Ethics, and Church

Jean-Marc Ela, *African Cry* (Eugene, Oregon: Wipf and Stock, 2005).

Emmanuel Katongole, *Born from Lament: The Theology and Politics of Hope in Africa* (Grand Rapids, Michigan: Eerdmans, 2017).

Agbonkhianmeghe E. Orobator, ed., *The Church We Want: African Catholics Look to Vatican III* (Maryknoll, New York: Orbis Books, 2016).

Diane Stinton, *Jesus of Africa: Voices of Contemporary African Christology* (Maryknoll, New York: Orbis Books, 2004).

Elochukwu Uzukwu, *A Listening Church: Autonomy and Communion in African Churches* (Eugene, Oregon: Wipf and Stock, 2006).

Index